TRADE UNIONS AND SOCIETY

Some Lessons of the British Experience

TRADE UNIONS AND SOCIETY

Some Lessons of the British Experience

John T. Addison and John Burton
Series Editor: Michael Walker

THE FRASER INSTITUTE
1984

The Fraser Institute is pleased to acknowledge financial support from the Max Bell Foundation and the Earhart Foundation for the project series, Unions and the Public Interest.

Canadian Cataloguing in Publication Data

Addison, John T., 1946 —
    Trade unions and society

(Labour market series ; 3)
Includes index.
ISBN 0-88975-056-4

1. Trade-unions. 2. Trade-unions — Great Britain.
I. Burton, John, 1945- II. Fraser Institute (Vancouver,
B.C.) III. Title. IV. Series.
HD6483.A33   331.88   C83-091486-2

Printed in Canada.

CONTENTS

PREFACE: Dr. Michael Walker xi
The Fraser Institute

ABOUT THE AUTHORS xxvii

CHAPTER ONE

THE BRITISH DISEASE AND TRADE UNIONISM:
CONVENTIONAL WISDOM AND POLITICAL
ECONOMY 1

I. INTRODUCTION 1
   Britain's Golden Age 1
   The decline.. 1
   The dimensions of Englanditis 2
   British disease is widespread 4
   Unions as the cause of the British disease 5

II. THE NATURE OF THE BRITISH DISEASE 6
   A variety of diagnoses... 6
   Symptoms 6
   The British disease in Britain 7
   The epidemiology of the British disease....................................... 7
   The bacillus spreads 8

III. TRADE UNIONS AND THE BRITISH DISEASE............................ 9
   A. Trade Unions and Inflation.. 10
      The weight of evidence 10
      Unions as a fundamental cause of inflation 11
   B. Trade Unions, the Political Market, and the Demand and Supply
      of Inflation... 12
      Union "rent-seeking" 12
      (a) Via union cartels 12
      (b) Via political pressure 14
      Unions versus taxpayers 15
      Political rent-seeking may produce inflation 16
      The inflation-tax-redistribution route 16
   C. Trade Unions and Unemployment 17
      Do unions cause unemployment?... 17
      Union power plus barriers equals unemployment........................ 18

D. Trade Unions and Economic Efficiency and Growth...................... 19
   Trade unions and Britain's slow growth 19
   (a) The static allocative inefficiency effect 20
   (b) The static X-inefficiency effect... 20
   (c) The trade union impact on growth performance...................... 21

IV. CONCLUSIONS AND CAVEATS... 22
   Some caveats... 23

CHAPTER TWO

TRADE UNIONS AND INFLATION.. 25

I. INTRODUCTION.. 25
   Different kinds of causes... 25

II. UNIONS AS THE DIRECT CAUSE OF INFLATION...................... 26
   Unions as passive element?.. 26
   Unions as the driving force... 26
   A. Union Power as a Cause of Inflation.. 27
      Has union power increased fast enough? 27
      Is bargaining power an independent cause of inflation? 27
      Public sector union power exception to the rule........................ 28
   B. Union Militancy as a Cause of Inflation 28
      Militancy and union membership... 28
      Strikes as a measure of militancy.. 30
      Different channels of influence.. 30
   C. Union Spillovers as a Cause of Inflation 30
      Wage norms and imitation... 31
      Union Politics... 31
      Flimsy theories?... 31
      Union politics — a more appealing explanation?...................... 32
      Wage setting imitation does occur.. 32
      Wage leadership explanations 32
      Spillover agnostics... 33
      Spillovers to the nonunion sector — union threat 33
      Minimum wages and spillovers.. 34
      Unions gain at expense of other workers 35
   D. Spillovers in the Public Sector.. 35
      Qualifications 36
      Evidence on the completeness of the monetarist explanation 37
      The multi-period wage contract and inflation............................ 37
      Long-term contracts and employers' interests 38
      Long-term contracts and unions 38

III. UNIONS AS FUNDAMENTAL DETERMINANTS OF INFLATION .. 38
  The fundamental cause of inflation 39
  Unions as a determinant of excessive money supply expansion 39
  Evidence on the political economy of inflation 41
  Political games and the money supply 43

IV. CONCLUSIONS 45

CHAPTER THREE

UNIONISM, PRODUCTIVITY AND GROWTH 47

  I. INTRODUCTION 47

  II. BRITAIN'S RELATIVE PRODUCTIVITY AND GROWTH RECORD .. 48
    A long-standing problem 48
    Isolating the role of unions 49
    International comparisons of union effects on productivity 49

  III. PRODUCTIVITY IN THE UNION AND NONUNION SECTORS 52
    A. Two Views of the Effect of Unions on Productivity 52
      The usual view 52
      The new view 53
      Benefits of collective action 54
      Shock effects of unionization 54
      Difficulties with the new view 55
      The statistical evidence 55
      Challenging conventional wisdom? 56
      Four serious flaws in Harvard studies 56
      Contradictory evidence from the U.K. 58
      Contradictory evidence from the U.S. 59
      Union effects on productivity — a wider sample 59
      Unions hurt competitive firms more 59
    B. Evidence on the Productivity Reducing Effects of Unions
      in the U.K. 60
      Buying out of low productivity 60
      Incomes policy spoils the option 61
      Productivity buy-out — a sound principle? 62
      Productivity in the public sector 62
      A generalized buy out of union 'bads'? 63

  IV. THE ROLE OF THE COLLECTIVE BARGAINING SYSTEM 64
    Productivity effects less in North America than the U.K. 64
    Occupational striation 65

  V. HOW BRITISH IS THE BRITISH DISEASE? 66

CHAPTER FOUR

**CORPORATISM — POWER SHARING BETWEEN BUSINESS, LABOUR
AND GOVERNMENT** 71

I. INTRODUCTION — THE MODERN STATE SHARES ITS
DECISION MAKING 71

II. THE CASES FOR AND AGAINST JOINT DECISION-MAKING 72
A. The Case For.. 72
Relativities and free riders.. 72
Equity and wage restraint... 73
The socio-political case 75
The growth of the New Industrial State 75
Unions need their share of political power.................................. 76
Inflation — a problem of under-regulation?................................. 76
But the proximate cause of inflation is still excess
money supply growth 77
The empirical side of socio-political explanations........................ 77
The larger the union the greater its social interest?...................... 77
B. The Case Against 78
The economic arguments once more... 81

III. THE SOCIAL CONTRACT 83
A corporatist experiment 83
Social contract breaks down 84
A legacy of law tailor-made to union demands............................. 85
A mushrooming of the closed shop 85
Management complicity... 86
Management opposition to "Industrial Democracy" 87

IV. SOME EMPIRICAL EVIDENCE ON CORPORATISM, STRIKES
AND INFLATION... 91

V. CONCLUSIONS AND WIDER REFLECTIONS 97

CHAPTER FIVE

**MARKET SYNDICALISM — "INDUSTRIAL DEMOCRACY"
AS A SOLUTION**.. 101

I. INTRODUCTION 101
A. The Interest in Industrial Democracy 101
Industrial democracy 101
A pervasive notion 101
In the Soviet bloc 102
An idea whose time has come?.. 102

B. Workers Self-Management: An Economic Perspective 103
Five features of market syndicalism 103
Industrial democracy in Western Europe 104

II. ARGUMENTS FOR MARKET SYNDICALISM 104
A. Introduction 104
Sharing power 104
Some problems with "tyranny of the majority" 105
WSM and alienation 106
The consumer interest 107
B. Economic Arguments: Market Syndicalism as a Cure for the
British Disease 107
Vanek's position 107
Jay's case 108
The Jay thesis 108
Solving the vicious trilemma 108
Unionism 'withers away' 110

III. MARKET SYNDICALISM AND THE PROBLEM OF PRODUCER
GROUP POWER 110
A. Union Power Transformed 110
Reasons why there would be no 'withering away' 111
Some puzzling facts about firms and syndicalism 112
B. How Do New Firms Arise in Syndicalist Economies? 113
Artificial versus natural emergence 113
The impossibility of collective entrepreneurship 113
Trade unions as the source of new firms 113
Entrepreneurs as the source of new business 114
WSM dissipates the return to entrepreneurship 115
Let the state pay the entrepreneurs 115
Could the workers pay the entrepreneurs? 116
Syndicalism will increase market power 117
C. WSM No Escape from Problems of Union Power 117

IV. MARKET SYNDICALISM AND THE BRITISH DISEASE 119
A. Inflation Under Market Syndicalism 119
Yugoslavia — the proof of the pudding 120
Industrial democracy amplifies Yugoslavian inflation 121
The political marketplace — a missing analytical link 122
B. Unemployment Under Market Syndicalism 122
Depends on other aspects of the economy 123
Wage maximization would reduce employment 123
Yugoslavian pudding again 124
C. Growth Under Market Syndicalism 125
Entrepreneurship or taxes the secret of WSM success 125
WSM retards growth and change 126

V. SOME GENERAL CONCLUSIONS 126
    Syndicalism no solution 126

CHAPTER SIX

**CAPITALISM, DEMOCRACY AND THE PROBLEM OF ORGANIZED
SECTIONAL INTERESTS** 129

I. VISIONS OF THE DEMISE OF CAPITALISM 129

II. THE SIMONS' THESIS: THE DESTRUCTION OF CAPITALISM
   AND DEMOCRACY BY UNIONISM 130
    A little-known analysis.. 131
    Abusing the economic powers of unions 131
    The strike threat strangles industry.. 131
    Unions cause the disruption and extermination of industry............. 132
    The problem of turning back the clock 133

III. THE CRITIQUE OF SIMONS' ANALYSIS: THE COLLECTIVE
    VOICE VIEW OF UNIONISM.. 134
    Cartel effects offset by benefits? 135

IV. A CRITIQUE OF THE TWO ANALYSES.................................... 136
    Three problems with Simons and the Harvard School.................... 136
   A. The Underlying Theoretical Model of the Trade Union.................. 137
    Do unions represent their members?...................................... 137
    A curious lacuna... 138
    Problems with democracy within unions...................................... 138
    The costs of monitoring union leadership..................................... 139
    Unions may not be representative 140
   B. The Importance and Significance of Market Responses
    to Unionism.. 140
    The market curbs monopoly power 140
    Four escape routes from labour monopoly 141
    Foreign competition 141
    The sunbelt... 141
    Employee substitution 142
    Decertification 142
    Do unions really contribute to the firm's welfare?........................ 142
    Mistakes and central inconsistencies in the Harvard view 144
   C. The Role and Significance of Union Activity
    in the Political Market... 145
    Unions in the political market — damming up the escape routes...... 145
    Simons' analysis reverses the market causality............................ 147
    Political process ignored by the Harvard school 147

V. CONCLUSION... 149
   NOTES 155
   REFERENCES 165
   INDEX.. 185

PREFACE

I. INTRODUCTION

The 1980s will undoubtedly be a time of great institutional change in Canada. As Canada, along with other western nations, attempts to deal with the reality of the changed political mood which is sweeping the globe, many of the practises and legislative provisions of the past will be modified. One of the most vexing challenges which faces Canadians is to devise a conception of the role of trade unionism appropriate to the refurbished institutional arrangements.

The purpose of this book is to derive understanding about the potential future role and effects of unionism in Canada by studying at a distance the trade unionism of the United Kingdom. The reason for examining the U.K. experience is that the British economy has been a kind of laboratory for labour market experiments during the course of the last three decades. By examining in detail the kinds of problems and solutions which have arisen there we may be better prepared to assess our own situation.

At one stage, this book was entitled "Trade Unions and the British Disease." The title was changed because of a concern that it would provide the misleading impression that the economic difficulties which have arisen in the United Kingdom are in some sense a uniquely British condition. It is one of the central contentions of this book that the forces which are found to be at work in Britain, producing the condition known as the British disease, are also found in all advanced western economies. Rather than regard themselves as exempt from the British disease, North Americans ought to regard themselves as potential sufferers and, therefore, to have more than passing curiosity about how the British situation has evolved and why.

Unlike the first book in this labour market series, *Unions and the Public Interest: Collective Bargaining in the Government Sector*, this is a book of essays written by two authors with very different styles. With much editing and revision this stylistic difference could have been eliminated to produce a more homogeneous whole. However, because of the differences in emphasis and approach which the authors have, the book would also have been less interesting — like a landscape without contours.

II. UNIONS AND THE BRITISH DISEASE

UNIONS AND INFLATION

The authors settled on a definition of the British disease which was first enunciated by the distinguished financial writer, Sam Brittan, as being a compound of sluggish economic growth, high inflation, and high unemployment. They then proceed to analyze the impact of unionism on all of these factors. In the first chapter John Burton surveys the conventional wisdom about the impact of unions on inflation, employment, and growth and provides a suggestion of an alternative explanation in the non-economic impact of unions via the political marketplace. Thus, for example, in Canada the political lobbying of the Canadian Labour Congress to have the federal government expand its social programs, the level and the extent of coverage of the Canada pension program, the amount of funding for medicare, advancement of money to Crown corporations, special employment programs, and so on, in the end causes the Government of Canada to spend more money than otherwise it might. If the Government of Canada does not collect enough taxes to pay for this expanded level of expenditures, a potential result is that more money will be created by the Bank of Canada to cover the ensuing governmental deficit. The end consequence of that is inflation.

UNIONS ONLY ONE SPECIAL INTEREST

However, in this inflation-causing role, unions are not alone. They are merely one of a vast number of special interest groups which in recent years have been able to make felt their opinions on the actions of government. What is true is that trade unions are well organized and are a particularly large group. Therefore, their effects are more obvious than the effect of other groups.

A similar special interest political model is applied by Professor Burton to the other aspects of the British disease — slow growth and high unemployment. In each case it seems clear that it is through the political marketplace effects of unions that we must look to find their ultimate impact on economic affairs. Professor Burton's chapter is by way of an introduction to a more complete analysis of each of these aspects of the British disease in separate chapters by Professor John Addison.

DO UNIONS MAKE THE ECONOMY INFLATION PROOF?

In Chapter Two, Professor Addison discusses the theoretical and empirical literature focusing on the linkage between trade unionism and inflation. Neither in the British case nor from other evidence, is he able to draw the popular conclusion that trade unions are a direct, proximate cause of inflation. Unions, it appears, do not push up the level of inflation by pushing up the level of costs, as is often implied. They do, however, on the basis of the evidence, seem to have an effect on how inflation moves through the economy and how rapidly the economy adjusts to increases and decreases in the inflation rate.

While exonerating unions as a proximate determinant of inflation, Professor Addison joins Burton in indicting them as a fundamental determinant along with other special interest groups. "Such groups have an implicit demand for inflation which vote-maximizing governments accommodate via the inflation tax," according to Addison, and while we are not yet in a position to precisely determine quantitatively the nature of that relationship there seems to be little doubt of its existence.

III. UNIONS, PRODUCTIVITY, AND ECONOMIC GROWTH

UNIONS INCREASE PRODUCTIVITY

In Chapter Three John Addison pursues the elusive relationship between unionism, productivity, and economic growth. He begins by the startling revelation that there is a considerable amount of evidence assembled by what he calls the Harvard School suggesting that unions actually increase the level of productivity in the economy. The reason advanced is that unions serve as a vehicle for expressing the collective view of workers. Where uniform work policies and shared working conditions involve an imposition of restrictions on individual behaviour, some sort of collective expression of the view of the workers harmonizes what would otherwise be a difficult working environment.

Also, in the view of the Harvard School, since work effort is often a shared responsibility requiring collective adherence to a work plan, the union can provide governance and other functions which will make the workplace operate more smoothly. In short, unions reduce the cost of bargaining because they provide a collective voice, they help rationalize the work structure, encourage the cooperation of the workforce, and in general make possible a more stable employment relationship between the employees and the employer.

PROBLEMS AND COUNTER-FINDINGS

Addison also surveys the empirical evidence provided by the Harvard School which supporters of that view find entirely confirmatory of the positive effects that unions have on productivity. Addison finds four serious flaws, however, in the Harvard studies relating both to the theory and to the estimation of effects. Moreover, he points out that there is also evidence pointing in the opposite direction. The work of Pencavel, for example, indicates that the unionization of the coal industry in the United Kingdom produced a 22 per cent reduction in the productivity of the workforce. Similarly, a recent study by Clark of 900 product line businesses in the United States, suggests that the impact of unionism on productivity is consistently negative.

UNIONS AS CATASTROPHE FOR EMPLOYMENT GROWTH

Clark's study also shows that unions have a very substantial effect on the profitability of firms, particularly small, highly competitive firms. In fact, he discovered that unions have virtually no effect on large firms in highly concentrated industries but a catastrophic effect of reducing profits by close to 40 per cent in the industries which are highly competitive and characterized by small firms. Given the recent estimates that more than half of all jobs created in the economy arise from small firms operating in the highly competitive service industries, the result strongly suggests that unions in the future can have a profound effect on the growth dynamics of all economies — but particularly the Canadian economy.

EVIDENCE FROM PRODUCTIVITY BARGAINS

According to Addison, the most pressing evidence of the effect of unions on productivity arises from the productivity bargains which have been struck between employers and employees. He cites, for example, the U.K. Standard Oil refinery case in which the company bargained for the relaxation of job demarcations, withdrawal of craftsman's mates, the provision for temporary and permanent shift working, and greater freedom in the use of supervision. Over the two year life of the agreement, output per man-hour rose by approximately 50 per cent and refinery overtime was reduced to 7.5 per cent from 18 per cent of total hours worked. In other words, unions were having a very distinct negative effect on the productivity of the installation.

In some sense, another more depressing result of Addison's survey is his determination that not only do unions have a negative effect on productivity, they also have a negative effect on the growth prospects for firms. Distressingly, most of this evidence arises as a by-product from the study of the effect of research and development activities on total factor productivity growth.

IV. THE GENERAL PROBLEM OF SECTIONAL INTERESTS

The first three chapters of the book amount to a telling case that trade unionism does indeed have many perverse economic effects. Trade unionism does have an effect on the rate of inflation. Trade unionism has reduced the levels of productivity in the U.K. economy and can be expected to have similar effects elsewhere. Trade unionism does reduce the rate of economic growth and, in particular, stymies the development and growth of small firms who provide the bulk of the growth of employment in North America. However, these revelations are the beginning rather than the end of the story because the analysis also discloses that trade unions are not the only sectional interest in society which has had these kinds of effects.

Trade Unions no less than the medical profession or the accounting profession have been successful in securing, via the political process, monopoly protections on their employment which have conveyed a disproportionate amount of economic power. The problem, therefore, is as complex as the multitude of balancing interest groups which go together to comprise a modern society. Most importantly, there is nothing peculiarly British about the concatenation of political and economic forces which these special interest groups can produce. It is just that the British have been playing at the game longer than anybody else.

However, it may also be true that the institutional setting in which the special interest game-playing occurs will have an effect on the outcome. Accordingly, in Chapters Four and Five, Addison and Burton investigate two potential solutions to the problem of power-sharing. The first, in Chapter Four, is the corporatism solution — what we in Canada have tended to dub tripartitism.

V. TRIPARTITISM

The corporatist solution first evidenced itself in the United Kingdom in then Conservative Prime Minister Edward Heath's offer to employers and unions to "share fully with the government the benefits and obligations involved in running the national economy." In that extension, Heath sought to blunt the anti-societal edge of special interests by enfolding them in the public interest.

CORPORATISM — A CURE FOR INFLATION?

In the particular case of inflation, corporatism is a solution to what has been regarded as the free-rider problem of competitive wage escalation. That is, the practise of each group in society to aggressively seek to advance their own wages without regard to the effect on others. The cooperative or corporatist solution provides greater transparency to the relative wage effects of aggressive bargaining by particular groups and, in the view of at least some analysts, provides an opportunity for the perception of equity to characterize the wage setting process.

OR, A SOURCE OF FURTHER DIFFICULTY?

The underlying motivation for the corporatist solution is the notion that by involving essentially self-interested parties in a communal process of determination, the destructive self-interest will be blunted. An alternative hypothesis has been explored by Burton and Addison in this monograph. Namely, that the problem arises essentially from the fact that special interest groups have been able to capture the political process and have been able to use it for their own purposes. Accordingly, a corporatist solution is likely to produce an even more malevolent outcome than the existing system because it would make it much easier for unions and corporations to gain concessions from government. In the ordinary scheme of things, unions have to use the standard political process and conventional means of political pressure to extract concessions from the government. In the context of a corporatist, co-determination solution to the wage growth problem, unions would be provided with direct bargaining power of a sort which at present they can only wish for.

THE SOCIAL CONTRACT

Addison's rendition of the experiment with the social contract in the United Kingdom provides strong evidence to suggest that corporatism is not the final solution to the problems presented by unionism. In tracking the British social contract from 1974 to 1978, Addison points out that it didn't work in controlling inflation, had apparently perverse effects on unemployment, and in the end left a legacy of changes in labour law which were virtually tailor-made to union requirements. The fact that many of the changes were supported by corporate interests, serves as a reminder that very often it is in the interests of management and labour to cooperate at the expense of the consumer.

The empirical record of corporatist solutions is neither extensive nor complete. In examining corporatist approaches to the problem of wage growth, inflation, and unemployment problems caused by sectional interests, the authors had, therefore, to be guided largely by analytical considerations. But, Burton and Addison's analysis is quite compelling — in fact, it is devastating. In their view, corporatism is really a magnification and extension of the problem of special interest groups which has already been identified as malevolent. It hardly seems fruitful to pursue a solution in that direction.

VI. INDUSTRIAL DEMOCRACY

A POPULAR NOTION

In Chapter Five, John Burton examines the notion of a labour-managed economy as an alternate system of economic organization. This is a timely analysis as ideas of profit-sharing, co-determination, worker participation, and industrial democracy have become quite popular in recent years. There is a perception by some that a labour-managed capitalist economy would be, in some sense, the media between the capitalism of North America and the centralized, authoritarian system typified by the Soviet Union. Yugoslavia, which is the most thoroughly developed labour-managed economy in the world, is an example of what some people seek in this regard.

Not surprisingly, this sort of solution has been widely canvassed in the United Kingdom. In 1978, as a reflection of this interest, the then-government placed legislation before Parliament which would have imposed a legal obligation on all companies employing more than 2,000 people to accept a minimum of one-third worker representation on their board of directors.

Even Pope John Paul II in his third encyclical Laborem Exercens called for fuller participation of workers in management.

WORKER DEMOCRACY — WHAT IS IT?

In turning to an analysis of industrial democracy or worker self-management, Burton is careful to distinguish that from the more commonly mentioned form of worker involvement in management which has legislative standing in some countries. The notion, for example, that firms should, as a compulsory matter, have a certain fraction of worker representation on the board of directors of a firm, is not so much worker self-management as it is an attenuation of the rights of the owners of the corporation. The directors of a corporation represent those who own the capital of the corporation. The arbitrary appointment of workers to fill some fraction of these positions effectively limits the extent to which the board of directors would take into account the interests of the capital owners.

ACCORDING TO JAY, THE ONLY WAY OUT?

Worker self-management has been proposed as a solution to the multiple ailments of the British disease. The British economist and pundit, Peter Jay, has argued, for example, that worker self-management may be the only escape route from the union-based, secularly-increasing problem of stagflation that has beset advanced western nations. While accepting the basic monetarist argument that inflation is caused by escalation of monetary growth, Jay argues that unions have had the effect of drastically escalating the natural rate of unemployment at which inflation occurs. As governments seek to maintain unemployment below the natural rate, the result is inflation. Accordingly, union monopoly is an underlying cause of the current inflation in the west and particularly in Britain.

Jay holds that it is not feasible to consider the dismantling of union monopoly power — worker self-management is the only escape route. His reasoning is that only under such a system will workers be forced to face and accept as constraints the market realities that confront employers in the western economies. Jay goes as far as to suggest that under a system of worker self-management, because the interests of workers and the firm will become one and the same, that unions would, in effect, wither away.

It was against this possibility, Burton points out, that a much more likely outcome is that unions would gain control of the means of production and simply transfer their special interest-seeking into the product market from the labour market and, hence, would in effect conspire against the consumer interest to raise prices. This possibility is particularly pronounced for unions controlling key installations in the economy such as power, courts, and other facilities whose shutdown due to strikes would disrupt the entire economy. A second and more important consideration, according to Burton, is the fact that under a system of worker self-management the essential competitive element in the capitalist society would be destroyed, namely, the constant effort of entrepreneurs to make profit by establishing new firms, producing new products or old products in a different or cheaper way.

The latter difficulty with worker self-management also points to a curious fact that in spite of the absence of legal or organizational prohibitions preventing the establishment of worker self-managed firms at the moment, very few have arisen in western economies. If worker self-management or worker enterprises are the solution to any problem, why is it that they have not emerged in profusion under capitalism?

THE PROOF OF THE PUDDING — YUGOSLAVIA

In the Yugoslavian case where worker self-management is the rule it has been observed that the number of enterprises has steadily declined and the birth rate of new firms has been much lower than the combined death and merger rate of existing enterprises. As a Yugoslavian economist has recently put it: "We are realizing more and more that entrepreneurship cannot be avoided in a modern economy and in order to get it, you have to pay for it." As a result, the Yugoslavian government has had to offer special incentives to entrepreneurs involving what amounts to the possibility of making profits in order to ensure the evolution of new firms. But even that provision has not been successful.

The conclusion, therefore, seems to be that worker self-management provides no escape from the problems of union power and will probably lead to an increased difficulty with producer group power. Neither does the worker self-management route appear to provide a way out of the British disease. Yugoslavia has typically experienced an inflation rate double or treble that of major capitalist, liberal democracies. In effect, the Yugoslavian experience suggests that worker self-management may ultimately lead to a more direct linkage between union power and inflation.

> A common experience is that of workers in a Yugoslavian enterprise awarding themselves a large pay raise. . . their enterprise then gets into liquidity difficulties and. . . the public authorities are subject to political pressures to keep the lame ducks afloat. Though the national bank tries to operate an anti-inflationary policy, it too finds itself obliged to expand the money supply enough to make this possible. . . .
> In British terms, it is as if bankrupt firms could rarely be closed, not merely in problem areas like Glasgow or South Wales, but even London or Coventry.

In other words, the central bank in Yugoslavia is forced by political pressure to act as a kind of lender of last resort to the lame-duck, worker-controlled enterprises which, consequently, are maintained by the proceeds of an inflation tax.

Neither does the experience of Yugoslavia suggest that market syndicalism is the solution to the problem of unemployment.

> . . . unemployment in Yugoslavia has been very high, even according to published official statistics, for many years. The ratio of vacancies to unemployment has consistently been the lowest of any OECD country. The migration of Yugoslav workers to the freer economies of western Europe has been one response to the sparseness of job opportunities.

It seems clear from an analysis of principle and on observation of practice that market syndicalism is likely to be the source of further difficulty rather than a solution to the joint problems characteristic of the British disease. Nevertheless, there is a widespread demand for this kind of solution in the western democracies as people claim, on grounds of "social justice," the liberation of man or for other reasons that there should be more involvement of workers in management. Burton's analysis suggests that it is to be hoped these efforts are unsuccessful.

VII. THE DEATH KNELL OF CAPITALISM

The analysis in this book does not contain a very promising outlook for the modern capitalist democracies. There seems imbedded within the democratic process itself a genetic defect which finds its expression in the untrammelled growth and development of special interest groups — one of which, unionism, will strangle the economic process. None of the solutions which analysts have found promising stand up to the test of careful scrutiny. It seems highly unlikely that an accommodation can be reached.

In the final chapter of the book John Burton confronts this inevitable decline thesis through the little-known work of H.C. Simons. One of the founders of the Chicago school of economics, Simons was, as early as the mid-1940s, predicting the emergence of "an awful dilemma" in capitalist, liberal democracies such as America, Britain, and Canada. These countries have allowed and, indeed, fostered by the governmental granting of illegal immunities, the emergence and growth of a large and powerful trade union movement. Simons' fears for the future were based on his analysis of the consequences of the abuse of the economic powers of a fully-matured union movement both in the economic and political arenas.

A CASSANDRAISH FINALE?

Simons' concern was based on two aspects of unionism: the strike threat power, conveyed to unionism by tolerant legislation, which he felt would lead to economic breakdown; and the monopoly power of unions which, in his view, would lead to the systematic extermination of industry by excessive labour costs. The Cassandraish finale of Simons' thesis was that even though unions would continue to be a minority of the population, it would be impossible for the majority to impose its will through the political process. The reason is that the union movement is a mass minority with the organizational ability to oppose a reformist, democratic government even if the latter is backed by an electoral majority or even a majority of the population. As Simons put it: "Democratic governments appear to be nearly impotent to enforce laws against mass minorities, even if majority opinion permitted it."

The problem for democracy is that once legislatures have given occupational monopolies to unions and other groups, it becomes very difficult to remove them. But removal of the monopolies may be essential for the maintenance of the economic order upon which a smoothly operating democracy depends. Again, in Simons' words, "Here, possibly is an awful dilemma: democracy cannot live with tight occupational monopolies; and it cannot destroy them, once they attain great power, without destroying itself in the process."

Against this analysis, Burton cites the Harvard School analysis, previously considered by John Addison, which opines that unions have a positive and not a negative effect on society's output and that, therefore, the dismal view of Simons is not warranted. There is, however, little evidence which stands up to scrutiny in support of the Harvard view and both Burton and Addison have tended to reject it.

All is not lost, however, because Burton is able to set aside Simons' chilling analysis. He does so by showing that Simons has underestimated the power of the market process to "defuse the problem of monopoly, including labour market monopoly." In the natural course of events, the creation of a monopoly creates an equal and opposite incentive for its destruction. Consumers abused by a market cartel have every incentive to reward firms who operate to buck the monopoly. Thus, markets destroy monopoly and consumers escape capture by producer groups.

THE ESCAPE FROM UNION STRANGULATION

In general terms, a society can avoid the problems of union monopoly by four basic escape routes. All of these are in evidence in the current situation in North America. Foreign competition provides a cheaper substitute for domestically produced, highly unionized products. Employers move away from high unionization towards areas of low unionization such as the escape from the frost belt states to the sun belt states in the United States. Thirdly, businesses have substituted types of employees with a lower propensity to unionize. As a consequence, the fraction of the total labour force unionized, at least in the private sector, has been declining. Fourth, there is the process of decertification within which union members themselves escape economic oppression by decertifying from their union.

UNIONS DAM UP THE ESCAPE ROUTES

A potential difficulty with this sanguine view of the market escape process, however, is the fact that by operating in the political marketplace, unions can short circuit the escape process. In fact, it is usually to inhibit market escape that unions put pressure on government to change the legislation by which they are governed. Secondary picketing, hot declarations, non-alliance clauses, successor rights, lobbying for import quotas, minimum wage laws, tariffs, and other restraints of competition are some of the ways in which the union movement attempts to cut off the market escape process. The essential point to be noted is that the only way that unions can be effective in thwarting the natural economic process which would tend to eliminate their power is by using the political process.

THE GREAT SOCIAL STRUGGLE

The other thing that is amply clear from the analysis is that trade unions are not the only organized sectional interests involved in the attempt to gather market power and to use the political process to short circuit the market escape process. As Burton puts it, "Two vast social processes are thus in constant clash with each other throughout time: the constant attempt of producer groups to make consumers captive through regulations issued and enforced by the state, and the market escape process."

In the end, Burton concludes the whole clash between special interests and market escape may become so counter-productive that by general agreement there will be a change in the basic rules under which the game is conducted so that the economic process is renewed and ultimately protected from destruction. Something along these lines may be at the moment happening in western society. Certainly in the United Kingdom there seems to have been an implicit social contract struck between the government of the day and the population that the time has come to make some basic changes to the way in which that society operates. Some of those changes relate to the powers which will be given in the future to organized labour and to other special interest groups.

As we in North America begin the process of examining the state of our institutions, it may well be that we also will have to consider some restraints on the ability of special interest groups to use the legislative process to their own ends. The analysis of this book strongly suggests that the power of unions ought to be a prime candidate for early treatment.

The Fraser Institute is pleased to be able to publish this review of one of our country's most pressing problems. It gratefully acknowledges the financial support of the Max Bell Foundation and the Earhart Foundation in making our labour market studies series possible. However, because the authors' conclusions were arrived at independently, the views expressed may not conform singly or collectively with those of the Institute's members or funding agencies.

M.A. Walker
1984

About the Authors

JOHN ADDISON

John Addison was educated at the London School of Economics, where he received his Ph.D degree in 1971. Between 1973 and 1980 he was lecturer in economics at the University of Aberdeen (Scotland), after serving for a year as an economic adviser with the U.K. Office of Manpower Economics. In January 1981 he joined the Department of Economics at the University of South Carolina. He is currently Professor of Economics in that department and 'gastprofessor' at the University of Hannover (Germany).

He has published widely within the field of labor economics, including articles in the *Economic Journal*, *Oxford Economic Papers*, *The Manchester School*, *Applied Economics*, *Australian Economic Papers*, *Journal of Labor Research*, *Research in Labor Economics*, the *British Journal of Industrial Relations*, and the *Scottish Journal of Political Economy*, *inter al*.

He is co-author (with W.S. Siebert) of *The Market for Labor: An Analytical Treatment* (Goodyear, 1979) and author of *Wage Policies and Collective Bargaining in Finland, Ireland and Norway* (OECD, 1979).

Dr. Addison is a member of the Editorial Board of the *Journal of Labor Research* and of the Editorial Advisory Board of the *Journal of Economics and Business*.

His current research interests include the real effects of secular inflation and the effects of unionism on productivity.

JOHN BURTON

John Burton is presently Research Fellow at the Institute of Economic Affairs, London, England and Co-director of the Employment Research Centre, University of Buckingham, England.

After his postgraduate studies at the London School of Economics, John Burton was a lecturer in economics at Southampton University (1969-1970), Kingston Polytechnic (1970-1979), and the University of Birmingham (1979-1983). In the summer of 1981 he was a visiting scholar at the Heritage Foundation, Washington D.C. for whom he wrote *The Political Future of American Trade Unions* (1982); and in 1981-1982 he was a Nuffield Foundation social science research fellow. His contributions to this volume were written during the tenure of the latter fellowship, the purpose of which was to apply some developments in modern microeconomics, including public choice analysis, to the study of unionism.

He has acted as a consultant to the Organization for Economic Cooperation and Development, and to several government bodies and private enterprises in the United Kingdom.

John Burton has published widely in the learned journals. His books include *Wage Inflation* (Macmillan, 1972); *The Job-Support Machine* (Centre for Policy Studies, 1979); *The Trojan Horse: Union Power in British Politics* (Adam Smith Institute, 1979), and *Picking Losers – The Political Economy of Industrial Policy* (Institute of Economic Affairs, 1983).

The authors wish to thank Professor B.C. Roberts of the London School of Economics for his helpful comments on an earlier draft.

CHAPTER ONE

THE BRITISH DISEASE AND TRADE UNIONISM: CONVENTIONAL WISDOM AND POLITICAL ECONOMY

John Burton

I. INTRODUCTION

BRITAIN'S GOLDEN AGE

Just over one century ago, in the middle of the nineteenth century, Britain was the predominant exporting nation in the world's economy. Britain also produced two-thirds of the world's energy, and the City of London was the undisputed centre of world finance. The dynamism of British manufacturing was then without parallel. It was the 'workshop of the world;' Britain then produced half of the world's total output of cotton cloth and of iron.

Subsequently, the predominance of the British economy was to become eroded. This was inevitable. The paramountcy of the British economy in the mid-nineteenth century was the simple consequence of the fact that this was the first country to show the capacity for continuous and self-sustaining economic growth: the world's 'first industrial nation,' as the historians often put it. The industry was a consequence, not a cause, of the possibilities of economic progress, and the leading quality of the British economy in the first half of the nineteenth century was not some matter of chance.

THE DECLINE

Britain was the first country to entertain considerable deregulation of the economy, and thus to set the stage for the evolutionary forces unleashed in an environment of free enterprise and free trade. Britain's 'industrial revolution' was a market revolution (just as those of Hong Kong and Singapore are today). However, it was predictable that other entrepreneurs in other similarly-placed countries would learn lessons from the new methods of organization and production first tried in Britain. A catching-up — perhaps even some over-taking, here and there — was inevitable, most especially in the relatively free economies of North America, where entrepreneurship also had the possibility of flourishing in profusion.

However, the sheer size of Britain's relative economic decline since the middle of the nineteenth century has been little short of catastrophic. Being a major participant in two World Wars doubtless involved "considerable" opportunity costs to Britain. However, other countries (such as France, America and West Germany) were also so involved, and their living standards are now well in advance of the general standard of living in the U.K. Phrases such as "England-itis," "The British Disease," "The English Sickness," and the "Sick Man of Europe" have been coined to describe this relatively poor performance of the British economy in the contemporary era.

THE DIMENSIONS OF ENGLANDITIS
It is in the post-war period that Britain's dramatic relative decline has become starkly apparent, and most noticeably so in relation to the economic performance of its major continental partners in the European Economic Community (EEC), France and West Germany. Even by as late as the mid-1950s Britain was still the foremost European power, in terms of both its economic power and military capacity. It was also far in advance of all other European countries in certain high-technology areas, such as the development of atomic energy. Since then the British economy has fallen unremittingly behind that of its major European partners. The figures presented in Table 1.1 tell their own story.

The "economic miracles" of France and West Germany in the 1950s and 1960s, compared to the lacklustre performance of the British economy, were doubtless a contributory factor in the decision of successive British gov-

2

Table 1.1

Comparative Growth of GDP since 1954
(based on figures in U.S. dollars at 1970 prices
and 1970 exchange rates)

	1954	*1960*	*1977*
Britain	100	117	175
France	100	133	297
Germany	100	164	310

GDP per capita (U.K. = 100) since 1954
(bases as above)

Britain	100	100	100
France	93	103	141
Germany	93	121	146

Growth of Productivity since 1954
(bases as above)

Britain	100	116	168
France	100	131	266
Germany	100	140	277

Share of Manufactured Goods exported by OECD Countries
(% at current prices)

Britain	18.9	15.0	8.5
France	7.2	8.7	8.9
Germany	12.2	17.4	18.8

Output per Man-hour in Manufacturing Industry, 1977
(pounds per hour)

Britain	2.70
France	4.50
Germany	7.10

Source: Henderson (1979).

ernments to apply for entry to the Common Market in 1961, 1967 and 1970. It was argued by pro-Marketeers that entry would bring a bracing tonic of competition to the British economy, leading to its rejuvenation. However, although the U.K. joined the EEC on January 1, 1973, the years since have passed without the appearance of a new British economic miracle. The English Sickness has continued.

A secret valedictory dispatch to the Foreign Secretary written by the then British Ambassador in Paris, subsequently leaked to the *Economist*, described expressively the continuing story of British economic decline in relation to its continental partners at the end of the 1970s:

> . . .today we are not only no longer a world power,. . . we are not even in the first rank even as a European one. Income per head in Britain is now, for the first time for over 300 years, below that in France. We are scarcely in the same economic league as the Germans or the French. We talk of ourselves without shame as being one of the less prosperous countries of Europe. The prognosis for the foreseeable future is discouraging. If present trends continue we shall be overtaken in Gross Domestic Product (GDP) per head by Italy and Spain well before the end of the century.[1]

BRITISH DISEASE IS WIDESPREAD
One objective of this chapter is to define and to clarify the nature and causes of the British disease. It is widely thought that the British disease is specific to Britain, the consequence of particular and insular British social or economic characteristics. I shall argue, to the contrary, that the British disease is a common ailment of the body politic, to be observed in many other countries. The United Kingdom is simply in a fairly advanced stage of the "disease." Second, I shall argue that although this "disease" has economic symptoms or consequences of a deleterious nature, the causes of it are not to be seen as emanating purely from economic factors alone. An understanding of the central role played by the political market is essential to the proper diagnosis of the British disease.

UNIONS AS THE CAUSE OF THE BRITISH DISEASE

A large and important segment of both British and external opinion would attribute the British economic malaise to the workings of a particularly important component of the contemporary British scene — the trade union movement or, more generally, the British industrial relations system. The British economist Arthur Shenfield has summarized the general flavour of this view:

What is the British disease, or perhaps better, what is it said to be? Self-destructive labour unruliness, evidenced by excessive wage demands, resistance to the advance of productivity, frequency of strikes and go-slows, unthinkingly malevolent attitudes of workers to employers combined with utter indifference to the interests of the community or of fellow workers or to their own long-term interests; all this leading to a lamentably poor national economic performance. Sometimes the diagnosticians add poor managerial performance as a major symptom, but it is the worker symptoms which are held to be the most prominent.[2]

The view that the union movement/the industrial relations system is at least responsible in part for the British economic malaise has been openly stated by some of the senior figures in all of Britain's major political parties. In 1969 the then (Labour) Premier, Harold Wilson, publicly committed himself to the view that certain reforms of the industrial relations system were vital in the interests of national economic efficiency. One decade later Sir Keith Joseph (subsequently to become the Secretary of State for Industry) published a pamphlet forthrightly entitled *Solving the Union Problem is the Key to Britain's Recovery*. [28] A large mass of less illustrious Britons also apparently maintain similar views, as the letters column of any British daily newspaper eloquently testifies.

What precisely is the role of the trade unions in the generation of the British disease? Are they the cause of it? The second objective of this chapter is to provide some answers to these questions. To set the scene for this task, the features of the British disease will first be examined.

II. THE NATURE OF THE BRITISH DISEASE

A VARIETY OF DIAGNOSES

There is a plethora of theories of the causation of the British disease, most notably as regards the sluggish growth aspect of it. Some analyses, for example, stress underlying sociological factors, such as the long-ingrained "cult of the amateur" in British society, resulting in a persistent failure to make profitable use of scientists and technology in British industry. [27] Other treatments of the phenomenon ascribe it variously to a low rate of investment induced by "stop-go" government policies; [42] a labour supply constraint on the expansion of British manufacturing; [30] the large share of non-marketed output in the British economy; [4] and even the inadequacies of economics itself as a foundation for growth policy. [31] All of these, and other, bold diagnoses of the phenomenon have been the subject of equally strong criticism in the literature.

SYMPTOMS

Much more accord is to be attained if we turn away from consideration of the nature of the British disease in a causal sense, and proceed by an examination of its symptoms. On this matter there is considerable harmony of opinion among economists. The first major symptom of the disease, on which all would agree, is that aspect emphasized in the Introduction to this chapter: sluggish economic growth. Others, such as Brittan, [7] would include a further phenomenon as symptomatic of the British economic malaise: the concatenation of high unemployment and high inflation commonly termed "stagflation." As Brittan also notes, these two maladies are not necessarily connected. The sluggish behaviour of the U.K. growth rate, compared to that of many other Western countries, is a phenomenon that dates back to the late nineteenth century. [33] [36] The emergence of stagflation in Britain is a much more recent phenomenon, dating from the 1960s. There is no necessary causal connection between the two phenomena of sclerotic growth and stagflation; one may occur without the other.

This chapter follows Brittan in defining the British disease as a compound of (possibly unrelated) economic maladies: sluggish economic growth, high inflation, and high unemployment. We turn now to a brief review of the facts on the British disease defined in these terms.

THE BRITISH DISEASE IN BRITAIN

First, British stagflation. The (measured) unemployment rate has been growing in the U.K. from the mid-Sixties. In 1962-1967 the annual average unemployment rate in the U.K. was 2.4 per cent; by 1976 it had reached 7 per cent. It currently (1983) stands at *circa* 15 per cent. Simultaneously, the British inflation rate has soared since the mid-Sixties — or, rather more specifically, since the 1967 Sterling devaluation. Over the period 1958-1969, the British inflation was creeping along at an annual average rate of 3.8 per cent; whereas from 1969 to 1977 the annual average rate was 12.6 per cent: a tripling of the trend inflation rate. In the second quarter of 1980, inflation reached a per annum rate of just over 20 per cent (but has subsequently slowed dramatically under Mrs. Thatcher to less than 5 per cent).

Second, the British growth performance. This has been relatively weak, compared to other major nations (which Britons still like to regard as their peers) throughout the post-war period, and extremely weak in the latter half of the Seventies. Over the two decades 1950-1970, the per capita real growth rate (real gross domestic product per head of population) in the U.K. was 2.3 per cent per annum, compared to an arithmetical average for 16 advanced, Western countries (including the U.S., Japan, and West Germany) of 3.8 per cent per annum.[3] The differences in these two percentages may seem small, but small differences in compound growth rates lead to large absolute differences when played out over decades (however, in 1980 and 1981 "Japanese-style" productivity growth rates were briefly recorded in the U.K.)

THE EPIDEMIOLOGY OF THE BRITISH DISEASE

It is not sufficiently well recognized, either by the British themselves or by foreign observers, that the British disease is by no means confined to the United Kingdom. The ordinary Briton, and indeed many British economists, are wont to identify the malaise as a specifically British problem.

Explanations are therefore sought and forwarded in terms of the peculiarities of the British social structure, culture, or economic history. Thus we have suggestions that the source of the problem in Britain lies in historically-embedded factors such as the "rigid" British class structure, the "cult of the amateur" in Britain, or the very fact that Britain was the first industrial nation (leading to contemporary "premature maturity"). Many other Western commentators are prone to agree with such British diagnoses. If the source of the malaise lies in something that is quite specific to Britain, then other countries cannot catch the infection. Thus many other Westerners comfort themselves with the notion that "it can't happen here."

There is, unfortunately, something very wrong with this comforting diagnosis of the British disease as a specifically British complaint. The British disease *has* been caught elsewhere — if not quite yet of epidemic proportions. This is true both of the sluggish growth and stagflation symptoms of the disease.

THE BACILLUS SPREADS
There has been a general weakening of the growth performance of the Western economies over the past decade. Although the British growth performance has been particularly sluggish, those of other Western countries have increasingly exhibited the same tendencies. Commenting on the period Hutton notes that:

> Almost as disappointing — though not absolutely and relatively as bad as our [British] growth and productivity record — have been, in these last 10 years, the performance of the United States, Germany, Italy, Scandinavia, Belgium, and, more recently, Japan and France. Something is rotten in the state of productivity, growth and employment in the leading Western countries, even if it is worst in our own country.[4]

A recent tendency towards stagflation is also a general phenomenon amongst Western nations, and is not at all confined to British shores. As Friedman [20] reveals, the plot of the five-year moving averages of inflation and unemployment in the Organization for Economic Cooperation and Development (OECD) countries since 1955 describes an upward-sloping "Phillips Curve." That is, throughout the West, over the past couple of decades, the trend rate of inflation and the underlying level of unemployment have risen secularly, together.

No other Western country may regard itself as immune from the British disease. The U.K. economy may exhibit the most advanced stage of the disease; but it has most certainly spread elsewhere.

III. TRADE UNIONS AND THE BRITISH DISEASE

What is the role of unionism in the three-horned British disease of high inflation, high unemployment, and slow growth?

To highlight the nature of the answer to this question developed here, it is useful to set up a straw man which may be called the "popular view" or conventional wisdom on the matter. By this I do not mean the mainstream academic economic opinion; indeed, it is impossible to talk of there being any consensus among economists upon such a matter so shrouded in controversy. Rather, by the conventional wisdom or popular view I mean the ideas on the role of unions in the British disease that are often to be found expressed by many ordinary Britons, and (some of) their political representatives. The main elements of this popular view may be itemized as follows:

1. On Inflation: Trade union militancy, or greed, or power, is a direct and primary cause of inflation. Trade unions force up money wages, labour costs, and thus generate price inflation. This is a characteristic man-in-the-street view of the inflationary process in Britain itself; street-corner monetarists are not in abundance (indeed, the vast majority would have little clear understanding of the term "monetarism").
2. On Unemployment: In relentlessly forcing up wages, trade unions cause not only wage inflation, but price their own members out of jobs. They are thus a contributory source of the unemployment aspect of the British disease.

3. On Sluggish Growth: By the forcing of restrictive practices and overmanning of enterprises, the trade unions have lowered productivity and throttled British growth.

In short, the trade unions are in Britain popularly ascribed with a direct, causal role in the generation of the British disease. In the following treatment I shall examine this view in detail, taking each facet of the British disease in turn. The conclusion, in brief, is that the popular view does not stand up well to close examination. However, this leads on to the forwarding of a different diagnosis of unionism's role in the British disease.

A. TRADE UNIONS AND INFLATION[5]
The popular view, in Britain, is that union wage-push is a direct — or, more technically, a proximate — cause of inflation. This particular aspect of the popular view does, it must be added, have the backing of a considerable body of academic economic opinion in Britain, in the form of the (primarily Keynesian) wage-push school of inflation theory. This includes such influential figures as Lord Kahn [29] and Sir John Hicks. [25]

THE WEIGHT OF EVIDENCE
However, the weight of the evidence, appertaining to a number of countries (including Britain), for various time periods, suggests that trade union pressure is not an identifiable proximate cause of inflation. It must be admitted, in stating this conclusion, that there are great difficulties in the proxying of concepts such as "trade union militancy" for the purposes of empirical testing. It may thus be that no one has yet discovered a good and plausible proxy for trade union "militancy" or "power." However, having entered this *caveat*, we must accept the weight of the empirical evidence as it (currently) stands. Our presently-available econometric evidence provides no robust support for the popular view that trade union pushfulness constitutes the proximate cause of inflation in Britain or other countries.[6] The evidence is more consistent with Friedman's assertion that 'unions are simply the thermometers registering the heat, rather than the furnaces producing the heat' [19] of inflation.

This is not to deny that trade unions affect the dynamics of the inflationary process. There is evidence to indicate, for a number of countries, (e.g. Thomas) [43] that the slope of the short-run (or "transient") Phillips Curve is steeper in the nonunionized sector of the labour market than in the unionized sector. Thus, apparently, wage changes are more responsive to variations in demand conditions in the former than the latter. The presence of unions seems to reduce the sensitivity of wages to swings in unemployment.

UNIONS AS A FUNDAMENTAL CAUSE OF INFLATION

The general conclusion is that while trade unions may influence the short-run trade off between inflation and unemployment, trade union pressure exerted directly in the market does not appear to be a proximate cause of inflation. However, it may be that union pressure is one of the fundamental causes of inflation — "the" or "a" cause of the monetary expansionism of government, which then leads to inflation. This is the proposition advanced by Hayek [22] [23] among others. To extend Friedman's analogy, the Hayekian view is that while unionism is not the "furnace" of contemporary inflation, it is the "bellows" fanning the flames of monetary expansion.

Thus it could be, to employ Gordon's [21] terminology, that the causation of inflation, at the fundamental level, lies in a 'demand for monetary accommodation,' or 'demand for inflation' exercised by the trade unions. Gordon argues that the unions are the main beneficiaries of inflation, and thus exert a demand for it in the political market, both directly (by lobbying) and indirectly (via the weight of their members' votes at election time).

There is, however, a central lacuna in the Hayek-Gordon thesis that trade union pressure is a fundamental cause of inflation, to which I have called attention elsewhere. [13] It is not clearly identified in their analysis how trade unions may gain from inflation, and thus the rationale for a union demand for inflation in the political market is left hanging in the air. Drawing upon my earlier work, [12] [15] I here advance a diagnosis of this matter.

B. TRADE UNIONS, THE POLITICAL MARKET, AND THE DEMAND AND SUPPLY OF INFLATION

UNION "RENT-SEEKING"

A trade union is a "rent-seeking" organization.† It seeks to redistribute income away from other members of society, towards the union, for the benefit of the union membership, or the union organization and administrators. As Stigler [41] has noted in his seminal economic analysis of the demand and supply of government regulation, there are two main potential avenues for such rent-seeking for any group, be it a group of firms, labour suppliers, or whatever. These are: the achievement of monopoly power in a pecuniary market via cartelization; and the gaining of the "assistance" of the state (cash, disbursements, the granting of favourable legislation, the use of governmental coercive powers, etc.) in the task of redistribution. To put it another way, rent-seeking takes place either through activities in pecuniary markets or in the political market. Any group, including trade unions, will choose to devote resources to these two avenues of rent-seeking according to the relative costs and returns of the two activities. We examine these, specifically regarding trade unions, in turn:

(a) Via union cartels

There are two main other types of income groups in the private sector, from whom trade unions may redistribute income, via cartelization, towards themselves: profit earners and nonunion employees.

The potential for redistribution from profits is rather circumscribed. Monopolistic rates of return in the product market are the exception, not the rule. Furthermore, the overall share of profits in national income is too small to provide much leeway for gains by the union movement. Phelps Brown has spelled this out succinctly:

---

†Editor's Note: "Rent-seeking" is a word used by economists to describe behaviour designed to increase the seeker's income above the norm which would be established in a competitive environment. In many instances this "rent-seeking" involves the installation of governmental impediments to normal market forces.

If the whole of the dividends and interest paid out by British companies in 1971 had been sequestrated and applied to raise pay *without any provision for those who have lost retirement incomes or trust and insurance funds*, average earnings would have been raised by less than 14 per cent; and this would have been once and for all (emphasis added).[7]

The more recent figures for the British economy would show even lower payoffs to a (once-over) profit-to-wage redistribution. The average rate of return on capital employed in the U.K. in 1982-1983 was one of the lowest ever recorded.

The alternative source of additions to union income via the exercise of union power in the pecuniary market lies in redistributing income from nonunion employees to unionized employees. That is, by restricting employment in the unionized sector — and simultaneously increasing the supply of labour to the nonunionized sector — unions may alter wage differentials in favour of their own members. The estimates of Johnson and Mieszkowski in fact

... strongly suggest that most, if not all, of the gains of union labor are made at the expense of nonunionized workers, and not at the expense of earnings on capital.[8]

I would argue that even these gains from nonunion workers are subject to great forces of erosion in the long run. First, the monopoly rents of trade unions, as with all monopolistic gains, become eroded by the escalation of the pecuniary price (e.g., entry fees) or time-price (e.g., over-lengthy apprenticeships) that unions need to impose on new members in order to restrict entry. Second, firms have incentives to switch to nonunion labour, and consumers to switch to the products of nonunionized firms. The monopoly rents achieved by trade unions are thus threatened, in the long run, as with all cartels, by the possibilities of substitution and the force of competition. Only if a union can get the state to step in and prevent such forces from operating (e.g., by the granting of a statutory monopoly) can the gains from cartelization be sustained in the long run.

The costs of effective cartelization are also likely to be large if a trade union has extensive membership, due to the costs of policing the labour cartel in such circumstances. The costs are likely to be relatively low in the case of small craft unions. The attraction of cartelization to a small union of craft workers is reinforced by the difficulties of substitution for such workers. According to the standard economic analysis of derived demand, the demand curve facing such workers will be more inelastic, and (other things equal) the potential for monopoly gain from successful cartelization the larger.

To conclude: the achievement of rent by trade unions via the cartelizing of markets is circumscribed by the small returns from "raiding" profits, and the long-run erosion of any rents so achieved arising from substitution and competition. The attraction of this avenue of rent-seeking would seem to be greatest to small unions of highly-skilled craft workers.

(b) Via political pressure
Although large numbers of members are at a distinct disadvantage in the construction of cartels, they are an equally strong advantage in the pursuit of rent via operation in the political market. A large number of members means a large amount of voting support potentially to be delivered to — or withheld from — the government. Thus rent-seeking via the political market is especially attractive to large trade unions.

Consider, for example, the case of the (currently) 230,000-strong National Union of Mineworkers (NUM) in Britain. Although the NUM has long operated a closed shop in the industry, it would be completely incapable of acquiring monopoly rent so long as the industry were open to competition; to new domestic nonunionized producers and to foreign competition. The NUM thus has the strong incentive to channel its rent-seeking activity via the political market. Specifically, it has the incentive to lobby for government subsidies to domestic coal production; for a statutory monopoly for the current producer (the National Coal Board) to prevent the dissipation of rent by the sharing of subsidies with new entrants; and for government protection against foreign competition. Those are precisely the policies that the NUM has long espoused: and to the desired effect. The British coal industry is now a nationalized statutory monopoly, in receipt of massive subsidies, and protected against low-cost foreign-produced coal.

All trade unions, and especially the largest, have the incentive to lobby in the political market for government expenditure for regulatory measures that redistribute resources from taxpayers towards the union organization or membership. This lobbying pressure is intensified in the case of industries or firms which historically have grown large (including large numbers of union members) but which are going into decline. Here, union lobbying typically takes the form of a demand for state subsidies, bail-out operations, or nationalization (such latter demands being an implicit demand for subsidization and/or protection).

UNIONS VERSUS TAXPAYERS
The taxpayers, who must ultimately foot the bill for such subventions, also constitute a lobby, a political resistance force against them. However, there are good theoretical grounds for arguing that producer group lobbying has greater influence on government than taxpayer resistance. [18] A producer works in one line of activity; the taxpayer funds a myriad of government activities. Furthermore, producers are often organized in formal organizations (trade unions, firms, employers' associations) and thus have the basic organizational apparatus to mount collectively-organized lobbying in the political market. Taxpayers are not organized into any union or organization, and any taxpayer that takes on the task of lobbying against producer group influence upon government would be providing a collective good for literally millions of other taxpayers. Thus every taxpayer has the incentive to act as a "free rider" in the provision of political resistance to producer group special pleading. We should therefore expect producer group, including trade union, lobbying for subventions and protection from government to be relatively intense, organized, persistent, and effective, while taxpayer lobbying resistance to such measures is weak and inchoate. Witness, for example, the difficulties that the Thatcher Government in Britain (and the Reagan Administration in the United States) is having in the task of reducing not the level but the *growth* of public spending — and most espe-

cially industrial subsidies (primarily, to nationalized concerns in the U.K.) — faced by massive special pleading and lobbying by the affected sectional interests.[9]

POLITICAL RENT-SEEKING MAY PRODUCE INFLATION

None of the foregoing analysis of union, or more generally, producer group, action in the political market *necessarily* implies a bias towards inflation. If governments were subject to a *constitutional* rule of a balanced budget, no inflation is likely to occur under such a scenario. Under such a rule, the outcome would perhaps be one where there was a higher level of (equal) taxation and government expenditure than that desired by the median taxpayer.

However, under a Keynesian fiscal constitution, it is possible for government to spend more than it raises in overt taxation. Under such a fiscal constitution, it has recourse to the creation of debt and of fiat money to finance its expenditure. The former form of finance raises interest rates (*ceteris paribus*), and directly harms important political constituencies — notably, those people holding (variable interest rate) mortgages and firms that are seeking to borrow. Witness, for example, the political difficulties that the Reagan administration is currently experiencing as a result of the high level of U.S. interest rates resulting from the high level of federal government borrowing.

THE INFLATION-TAX-REDISTRIBUTION ROUTE

The creation of money is attractive to government as a means of financing its expenditures due to the political problems attaching to overt taxation and to government debt creation. It has been realized for some time in the literature of political economy that inflation is a "hidden" form of taxation that furthermore (under current arrangements) does not require legislative approval.

Following Bailey, [5] the implicit assumption of the academic literature on the inflation tax — the tax on money-holdings created by issuance of government money — has been that inflationary finance is a means of redistributing resources from net money holders to the government, without recourse to explicit taxation. But these resources may then be redistributed to other groups. Inflationary finance may thus be an attractive instrument of redistribution (towards themselves) for powerful political groups.

Trade unions are not the only sectional interest groups involved in this "game" of redistribution via inflation. Other mass lobbies for redistribution via the state towards themselves also exist; for example, the householder lobby. Trade unions, however, are one of the most well-organized political lobbies, not least because they have been granted the legal powers by legislatures in the West to impose costs on employers who do not voluntarily choose to buy trade union services.

There are three points to be emphasized, by way of *caveat*, on this matter. First, trade union members and administrators do not have a direct interest in inflation. They have an interest in redistributing resources towards themselves, via government, and the inflation tax is one means of so doing. In this way, the incentive of trade unions to push for inflation in the political market arises. Their interest is indirect. Second, they are by no means the only group to seek to use this form of taxation, indirectly. Third, just as there is ceaseless change in pecuniary markets, so it is in the political market. Government is subject to a continuously shifting set of political influences, coalitions, and political demands.

The general conclusion is as follows. First, it would seem to be the case that large trade unions have an incentive to work through the political market to redistribute resources towards themselves, and there is an especial incentive (under a Keynesian fiscal constitution) to use the form of taxation called inflation for this purpose. Second, we should not expect to find a clear empirical relationship between union influence on the political market and monetary growth. The game being played in the political market is far more complicated. It is simply that trade unions are one of the principal players.

C. TRADE UNIONS AND UNEMPLOYMENT

DO UNIONS CAUSE UNEMPLOYMENT?
Do union-enforced, supra-competitive wage rates give rise to a higher level of unemployment?

According to economic theory they will not *necessarily* do so, in the long run. Certainly, if there is a step increase in the power of trade unions in labour markets, there will be a relatively sudden rise in union wage rates, and thus (eventually) a contraction in the demand for labour in the areas where this has occurred. This will throw certain of the previously employed into unemployment. The unemployment rate is likely to rise. However, so long as there are no barriers to expanded employment and *relative* wage reduction in the nonunion sector of the labour market, those displaced from jobs in the unionized sector will eventually be absorbed into employment in the nonunion sector. Thus, given wage flexibility in the nonunion sector, economic analysis predicts that a step increase in union power would lead to (a) a temporary boost to the unemployment total; (b) a long-run widening of the union-nonunion wage differential; and (c) no necessary effect on the long-run equilibrium rate of unemployment. Given the assumptions, trade union pressure on union-sector wages is not to be held responsible for the course of the long-run equilibrium rate of unemployment.

UNION POWER PLUS BARRIERS EQUALS UNEMPLOYMENT
However, government has embedded certain impediments to the downward adjustment of wages in the nonunionized sector of the British labour market. Principally, these are minimum wages which proscribe the legal minima that apply to various trades, covering some three and a half million workers, and the unemployment benefit/social security payments system. The latter creates also a floor to wages in the nonunion sector, and prevents the latter from absorbing the labour displaced by union wage mark-ups in the union sector. It appears that only a relatively small proportion of workers in Britain would be financially better off when unemployed. [3] In most cases the "replacement ratio" — the ratio of income (from government) out of work to that in work — is less than 100 per cent. However, wages cannot fall in the nonunion sector below the level of the replacement ratio *plus* the premium necessary to induce people to work. The replacement ratio in Britain (which varies with

family circumstances and the duration of unemployment) has generally risen compared with the first half of the Sixties. The floor on wages in the nonunion sector has thus risen.

Thus the conditions necessary for a growth of union power to generate a rise in the equilibrium unemployment rate — i.e., factors setting a floor to the wage level in nonunionized activities — are deeply entrenched in Britain. Evidence relating to both the market impact of trade unions [32] in Britain and their economic and political power [10] would suggest that there has in fact been a growth in union power over the last decade-and-a-half. It is likely, given the recently rising wage floors embedded in the nonunion sector of the British economy, that this development has raised the natural or equilibrium rate of unemployment in Britain.[10]

Clearly the unions are not directly responsible for this development. But for the existence of the wage floors, the growth of union economic power would not have caused a rise in the long-run, equilibrium rate of unemployment. However, it is the fact that trade unions, in Britain and throughout the West, have always been vociferous advocates of wage floors in the nonunion sector. Trade unions are so motivated, as Bloch [6] argues, because the existence of state-enforced wage floors in the nonunion sector reduces competition from nonunion workers. The wage floors are an essential adjunct to the successful maintenance of union monopoly power.

If trade union pressure is to be held responsible for the creation of unemployment, it is not simply their pressure on union wages that is the source of the problem. Their pressure applied through the political market for wage floors to prevent competition from nonunion labour is also an essential element of the picture.

D. TRADE UNIONS AND ECONOMIC EFFICIENCY AND GROWTH

TRADE UNIONS AND BRITAIN'S SLOW GROWTH

Are trade unions responsible for the sluggish growth performance of the British economy, as popularly supposed?

Here we must distinguish between three separate matters, often (vastly) confused in popular discussion upon the topic: the static allocative inefficiency effect of unionism, their static X-inefficiency effect, and the influence of unionism on the long-run evolution of efficiency in the economy.

(a) The static allocative inefficiency effect

The exercise of union power causes wages (and thus costs) to be higher than they otherwise would be in unionized industries, and lower in nonunionized sectors. This wage/cost/price distortion causes the output of unionized sectors to be lower than optimal, and the output of non-unionized sectors to be higher than optimal (or, if wage floors exist, for unemployment to result). This is the static allocative inefficiency effect of unionism.

Estimates suggest that this effect of unionism on efficiency is relatively small. Rees [39] and Johnson and Mieszkowski [27] have estimated that this welfare loss associated with this misallocation of resources amounts to only one-tenth of 1 per cent of gross national product, in the U.S.A. Estimates for the U.K. [9] are larger, but one still of small overall size.

(b) The static X-inefficiency effect

This is the effect of unionism on inefficiency in production (as against inefficiency in resource allocation) resulting from restrictive practices, over-manning, featherbedding, inefficient job demarcation, and so on.

We have very little hard evidence relating to this matter — despite its importance, and indeed its highly topical nature. Pencavel's [37] study is one of the few bits of serious estimation we have on this matter — and even this pertains to a very far-off time period. For what it is worth (as an indicator of the present situation), his study of productivity in the British coal mining industry 1900-1913 suggested that a totally-unionized coal-field would produce 22 per cent less than a (totally) nonunionized one, all other things being equal.

How much X-inefficiency results from restrictive practices in steel, the newspaper industry, British Rail, the docks, the General Post Office, the legal profession, and so on? We simply don't know. Rees's [39] guestimate was that in the U.S. the output loss from union featherbedding was at least as large as that from allocative inefficiency. This most important of questions has not been studied in any depth in Britain. Quantitative guestimates would therefore seem unwise.

(c) The trade union impact on growth performance.

The two effects discussed above are of a static nature. They refer to once-over effects on the *level* of efficiency. Even if large and negative (in terms of their effect on the level of efficiency) they would not necessarily affect the *rate of growth* of efficiency in the long run. But, if we are interested in explaining sluggish *growth*, it is this dynamical aspect that is of importance, not the static effects per se.

Professor Olson [35] has recently advanced an interesting public-choice theoretic analysis which throws light on this murky matter. His thesis is that the comparatively slow growth of the British economy is intimately related to the greater prevalence and significance in Britain of collectively-organized sectional interest groups — not only in the form of trade unions, but also professional associations, trade associations, and other lobbies and cartels.

Olson argues that the resulting market closure has had not only static (in)efficiency effects, but has also corroded the evolutionary mechanism of the British economy — its growth performance.

One thing that needs greater attention is the mechanism whereby this comes about. A tentative sketch of this matter is here offered.

As Alchian [1] has argued, a private enterprise economy, in which no government subsidies to industry exist, has a Darwinian "survival-of-the-fitter" aspect. Those enterprises which make positive profits survive, and perhaps grow; those enterprises which make losses are (eventually) evolved out via bankruptcy proceedings. New enterprises dealing in new products, or organized on different principles, are also continuously being created. Some survive; some do not. Thus the process of economic evolution occurs.

21

Producer groups have an incentive to lobby in the political market to get government to impair this process in their own interest. There is, for example, the incentive to get government to stifle the emergence of new competition. Again, there is a very strong incentive for enterprises which are making losses to lobby for government subsidization. These measures dampen the possibilities of economic evolution.

In Britain itself vast resources have been diverted to sustain loss-making nationalized concerns located, in particular, in the automobile, steel, shipbuilding, and coal mining industries. Large volumes of subsidies have also been given to a large variety of ostensibly private concerns. [11]

Trade unions are by no means the only producer interest group lobbying for such subsidies and other impairments of the process of economic evolution. Large private concerns and the Boards of nationalized industries have also been important players in this socially destructive game. The precise allocation of responsibilities among such interest groups is an interesting but unknown matter. All that is here alleged is that British unions have often been active participants in the process.

IV. CONCLUSIONS AND CAVEATS

This chapter has examined critically a popular view of the role of trade unions in the generation of the British disease. This conventional wisdom is that unionism is in large part directly responsible for the British disease. This deleterious impact of unionism is also seen, in the popular view, as exerted primarily through effects in the economic arena — on inflation, unemployment, and growth. This conventional view has been found wanting, both on theoretical and empirical grounds.

This is not to deny that trade unions do have economic effects. They clearly do exert direct influence in the economic arena. Trade unions evidently have effects on the level of (some) wage rates; they can also cause the displacement of labour by their wage policies. In this way also they may generate allocative inefficiencies. Furthermore, through restrictive practices they may in some industries cause X-inefficiency in production. However, it does not follow from this that the unions are directly responsible for the British disease. *Relatively* high union wages do not necessarily cause perennial inflation of all wages and prices. The *temporary* displacement of labour from one sector to another will not by itself cause a rising long-run equilibrium rate of unemployment. Such *static* inefficiencies in allocation and production as may be attributed to unions do not necessarily cause *dynamic* inefficiencies and sluggish growth.

Against this conventional view an alternative thesis has been advanced. The conventional wisdom is that unionism has in Britain directly caused the British disease via its effects in the economic arena. The alternative thesis tentatively sketched out in the foregoing is that the connection is more subtle. The contribution of trade unions to the British disease is indirect, and works through their activities in the political market, or the interaction of their economic and political impacts. To the extent that they are responsible for some part of the macro-economic phenomena we label as the British disease, British unionism would appear to be a fundamental, and not proximate, cause of the problems.

SOME CAVEATS
Some important *caveats* to this argument need reiteration. First, the unions are not the only organizations or lobbies involved in active pressurizing of the political arena for their sectional interests. Professional associations, the householder lobby, major corporations, employers associations, state pensioners (and so on) also constitute major implicit or explicit lobbies for government measures which promote their sectional interest. Trade unions are but one — even though a very important one in Britain — of the interest groups involved in this general process.

Secondly, the relative strength of union voice in the political market is likely to change over time. For both this and the foregoing reason it is improbable that we will find any neat quantitative relation between union pressure in the political market and government policies towards monetary growth, the budget deficit, wage floors, and lame-duck enterprises.

Thus the source of the British disease is to be seen in a general light. The causation of the disease lies in a maturing process involving the multiple and increasingly unrestrained pursuit of sectional interests in the political marketplace. Trade unionism is an important element, not the sum total, of this fundamental problem now facing the pluralist democracies of the West.

CHAPTER TWO

TRADE UNIONS AND INFLATION

John T. Addison

I. INTRODUCTION

DIFFERENT KINDS OF CAUSES

In Britain, as elsewhere, considerable controversy exists concerning the causal role of trade unions in the inflationary process. This debate may be made more transparent by distinguishing between the proximate and fundamental determinants. The proximate cause is the direct cause of an event but this proximate cause may itself have been the effect of another cause, termed the fundamental cause.

Monetarists, for example, emphasize the issue of proximate causation. They argue that inflation is simply the result of excessive money growth relative to the growth rate of output. If this argument is accepted, and it is accepted by most economists, the next problem is to ascertain what caused the money supply to expand in the first place. In other words, what is the fundamental determinant of inflation?

Distinguishing between proximate and fundamental causation in our analysis of trade union impact is at once both correct and expositionally convenient. It does however suggest rather more structure and coherence to the debate on union impact that is observed in practice. The strength of the distinction is that it will enable us to argue that trade unions are not a direct or proximate cause of inflation but may nonetheless constitute a primary fundamental cause or impetus behind the current inflation.

II. UNIONS AS THE DIRECT CAUSE OF INFLATION

UNIONS AS PASSIVE ELEMENT?
The basic monetarist position on proximate causation follows Friedman's[1] dictum that "unions are simply the thermometers registering the heat, rather than the furnaces producing the heat" of the inflationary process. On this view, unions have an essentially passive role, responding to but not motivating inflationary pressure. The origins of inflation are, then, to be sought in the monetary sector. An excessive growth rate of the money supply forces up prices and creates excess demand for both union and nonunion labour. The price increases feed into inflation expectations and further fuel wage advance in union and nonunion sectors, which in turn feeds back into prices. Despite the drama attaching to wage bargaining in the union sector, the wage determination process is said to be much the same as that in the nonunion sector. This conclusion is modified in a number of respects, principally to allow for the different mechanics of union wage determination (see below).

UNIONS AS THE DRIVING FORCE
In sharp contrast to monetarism, counter-orthodoxy (which Burton [10] labels the 'furnace' view of unionism's role in inflation) maintains that inflation originates in the labour market rather than in the monetary sector of the economy. Unions, so the argument runs, can affect the rate of change in wages and thereby, via increased costs, directly increase prices independently of demand. According to this view, the causal links in monetarist thinking are reversed. Wage inflation in the union sector creates unemployment and price inflation. The monetary authorities in the attempt to mop up the unemployment validate the wage and price increases with increases in the money supply. And, as with the monetarist explanation, the increase in the prices heightens inflation expectations, which feed back into wages.

    If furnace analysts, to use Burton's [10] terminology, discount the role of money, what are the determinants of wage change and hence inflation? Three main strands to the argument that unions are the motive force of wage and price inflation have emerged in the British context. These are the 'union power,' 'union militancy,' and 'union spillover' versions of the furnace approach. We next briefly examine each in turn before returning to what we consider to be the important, yet mechanical, effect of unions and other market institutions on the inflationary process, as viewed from the perspective of proximate causation.

A. UNION POWER AS A CAUSE OF INFLATION

Union's market power can also be affected via changes in the legislative framework which affect the costs of enforcing the union's monopoly. Increases in union monopoly power may be expected to increase the union-nonunion wage differential and lead to a one-time increase in the level of wages. Union monopoly power is reflected in the difficulty of substituting other inputs for union labour and low elasticity of demand for the product produced by union labour. The less sensitive the demand for union labour, the stronger is union power.

HAS UNION POWER INCREASED FAST ENOUGH?

For union monopoly power to lead to inflation there would need to be continuing increases in that power through time. There is some evidence to suggest that the monopoly power of British trade unions did increase in the decade of the 1970s as a result of legislation that reduced the cost of enforcing union monopoly (Chapter Four). There is also evidence that the union-nonunion differential increased substantially during the 1970s. [39] However, union monopoly power has not increased as rapidly or as consistently as would be required to explain postwar inflation in Britain. It can, nevertheless, safely be conceded that monopoly power can and has led to discrete upward movements in the level of wages from time to time. We may then speak of 'wage push' without accepting the union monopoly power thesis, since such events are the exception rather than the rule.[2]

IS BARGAINING POWER AN INDEPENDENT CAUSE OF INFLATION?

Union power can also be equated with bargaining power. However, empirical examination suggests that bargaining power is determined by ordinary economic variables such as the pressure of demand, prices, profits, and taxes.[3] To be accurate, the furnace view of reality requires that union behaviour be determined independently of economic variables. In practice, then, bargaining power theories may be viewed as an amplification of the standard monetarist interpretation.[4]

There are, moreover, no real signs that bargaining or strike threat power has increased secularly as the result of the process of economic development, at least within the private sector of the economy. This is largely because of the constraints on union pushfulness and management proneness to make concessions, the array of labour substitutes available in the advanced economy, and the fact that strike anticipations promote long and short-run adjustments that reduce vulnerability to the strike threat.

PUBLIC SECTOR UNION POWER EXCEPTION TO THE RULE

One can be less sanguine with respect to the public sector in general and nationalized industries in particular. In the latter, the high degree of union density, product market concentration, and degree of divorce between ownership (taxpayers) and control (politicians) do give rise for concern. We whall return to this question in the "Conclusions" to this chapter.

B. UNION MILITANCY AS A CAUSE OF INFLATION

Unlike the monopoly power version, this variant of the furnace analysis is concerned with the *subjective* propensity of unionists to indulge in wage push or, equivalently, the intensity of their mood for militant action in wage bargaining. The problem for analysts has been how to measure the degree of militancy.

MILITANCY AND UNION MEMBERSHIP

The principal approach has been to develop proxies for this attitudinal variable.[5] The most popular proxies have been constructed from measure of union membership. Thus in a series of papers the British economist Hines [29] [30] [31] [32] argued that the percentage of the labour force belonging to unions or union density[6] may be used as a proxy for militancy. The reasoning is that when unions are aggressive they will simultaneously increase their membership and push up wage rates.[7] Hines reports a positive relationship between British wage inflation and his proxy for militancy over various sample periods and for different levels of aggregation. He takes this evidence as providing unambiguous corroboration of the thesis that union militancy causes wage inflation; a result underlined by his finding that the degree of wage escalation did not seem to be affected by the overall level of demand in the economy.

Hines' analysis has been the source of continuing controversy in Britain. Part of this controversy arises from the observation that the average wage level is a weighted average of union and nonunion wages where the weights are determined by the degree of union membership. If union density increases and the union-nonunion differential is positive, then the average wage will increase, *ceteris paribus*.[8] Thus the Hines' result may simply reflect the fact that a weighted average changes when its weights change. Union militancy, as defined by Hines, has no behavioural content when viewed in this light.

This observation apart, there is the obvious point that Hines' model is not constructed from any well-developed economic theory of union behaviour but, rather, from the ad hoc proposition that the rate of change in union density is a reliable indicator of union militancy. At best, the variable possesses predictive power (see below) but not explanatory power.[9]

Indeed, the observed relation between wage inflation and union density might simply reflect a passive security motive. Thus one might argue that the greater the wage increase claimed by a union, the greater will be the probability of a work stoppage and the greater the incentive to join the union (assuming the union pays strike benefits). The demand for union membership may then rise *before* (and presumably fall *after*) wage negotiation bouts.

It has also been noted that Hines' militancy proxy does not predict well at the industry level using different data on unionization. [58] Be this as it may, the hypothesis does not appear to perform well outside Britain. [53] [56]

STRIKES AS A MEASURE OF MILITANCY
These and other difficulties, have led other analysts to experiment with alternative militancy proxies. The most common proxy has been strikes and the empirical results have been contradictory.[10] Such conflicting results stem in part from the fact that the relationship between the *chosen measure of strikes* and wage inflation is unstable. More fundamentally, the various studies suffer from the lack of a firm theoretical underpinning, and when such a framework is superimposed it often reveals that there is fundamental ambiguity about how strikes should affect wage change.[34] Again, it has been argued that an observed positive relation between wage inflation and strikes (and changes in union membership) is spurious, simply reflecting the joint determination of both variables by underlying economic forces.[11]

DIFFERENT CHANNELS OF INFLUENCE
Commentators sympathetic to the militancy argument have suggested that Hines has incorrectly identified the channel of that influence. Thus Mulvey and Gregory [43] argue that union militancy operates via the union-nonunion wage differential. This argument has a basis in the simple identity noted earlier, from which it can be seen that an increasing differential will inflate the average rate of change in wages.[12] Unfortunately, it is difficult to distinguish between the different types of behaviour postulated and the mere shuffling of identities. Thus the union-nonunion differential may fluctuate for a number of reasons, [54] and its level may affect unionization to a greater extent than the converse.

Note finally the curiously one-sided nature of the militancy explanation: no complementary analysis of employer behaviour is offered. The assumption is either that employer resistance has been reduced to insignificance in the postwar interval or that firms now tend to experience uniform wage increases that leave their competitive positions and market shares undisturbed. This assumed uniformity of wage increase brings us conveniently to the final variant of the furnace analysis.

C. UNION SPILLOVERS AS A CAUSE OF INFLATION
The central idea of the spillover hypothesis is that nominal wage changes are transmitted from one sector of the labour

market to another not by a market mechanism but by an imitative or spillover mechanism.

WAGE NORMS AND IMITATION
The theoretical basis of wage spillover is based on notions of relative deprivation and union politics. The relative deprivation hypothesis argues that if wage increases secured by some groups cause actual wage differentials to fall below the expected norms of other groups, then the latter will feel relatively deprived and will be led to restore the balance by demanding similar wage rises.

UNION POLITICS
The union politics hypothesis seeks more directly to explain the mechanism leading to the interdependence of pay claims. The basic idea is that if a union leadership fails to match the wage increases secured in other jurisdictions, rank-and-file disaffection will produce external and internal threats to that leadership, via membership loss and intra-union political challenge respectively. In consequence, so the argument runs, each individual union seeks 'competitively' to match the wage increases negotiated by others.

FLIMSY THEORIES?
Both of these explanations emerge, on closer inspection, to be remarkably flimsy constructs. The relative deprivation theory does not allow quantification of the 'stock' of relative deprivation. In consequence, the proposition that wage increases are determined by relative deprivation can not be directly tested against reality. Faced with this difficulty, researchers have employed indirect tests, seeking to infer reference group comparisons from data on wage changes. Unfortunately, such attempts to identify reference groups (or 'orbits of coercive comparison') involve after-the-fact rationalization of the data in terms of the theory. It is not surprising, therefore, that different analysts using much the same data sets and time periods have managed to isolate almost entirely contradictory reference sets or spillover patterns. [30] [49] Each set of evidence is of course consistent with an irrefutable theory!

UNION POLITICS — A MORE APPEALING EXPLANATION?

The union politics hypothesis has greater intuitive appeal because of its emphasis upon mechanisms. Yet it, too, must be viewed as unsatisfactory as a theory of wage inflation since it neglects labour and product market constraints. Employer resistance to uniform wage claims will likely vary across the labour market according to different product and factor market conditions. Moreover, wage formation in the nonunion sector is ignored. Even more fundamental a problem is the fact that the union politics theory does not explain how the 'going rate' of wage increase arises in the first place.

We need not dwell on the results of indirect tests[13] of the union politics hypothesis for the simple reason that British and other research has consistently failed to detect evidence of stylized wage setting behaviour in the form of 'wage rounds.' [19] [37] [38]

WAGE SETTING IMITATION DOES OCCUR

Having said this, there is evidence of wage imitation. But we should expect to find interconnections between wage changes in different sectors of the labour market due to the operation of market forces, even if a spillover process did not exist. (The determination of wages for a given firm is a function of all the usual demand and supply factors, the latter including the wage rates paid by *all* competing firms.)

WAGE LEADERSHIP EXPLANATIONS

Given the elusiveness of wage imitation theory, other analysts have postulated some form of wage leadership. That is, there is supposed to be a leading sector in the spillover system with which all other sectors/unions make reference comparisons. The introduction of a 'pace setter' provides the missing link in the causal chain and removes the ambiguity noted above, as to where the process ultimately begins. But this is not the end of the story for a number of reasons. First, there is still the matter of explaining wage determination in the leading sector. Second, the leading sector has to be identified. Unfortunately, in both cases analysts have resorted to blatantly ad hoc methods. For this reason the identity of the leading sector is either in dispute[14] or is apparently subject to abrupt shifts through time.[15]

SPILLOVER AGNOSTICS
Interestingly, the Canadian analysts Christofides, Swidinsky and Wilton [13] have advanced what might be termed an 'agnostic' spillover model. The nonspillover content of actual wage changes is assumed to be determined by more or less standard market variables, such as excess demand and inflation expectations. The spillover component is derived by defining a reference set along a number of dimensions (e.g. region and industry-region) and adding in past wage settlements according to each dimension until the explanatory power of the spillover variables is exhausted. Such spillovers add to a simple excess demand explanation of wage change, particularly that for the most narrowly defined industry-regional reference group. Yet the authors wisely note that spillovers may have a market interpretation — hence the agnostic tag. The superior performance of the most narrowly defined reference set appears to underline this.

So much, then, for spillovers within the union sector. Our conclusion must be that research on union spillover processes has failed to provide a satisfactory foundation for the view that trade unions are a motive force of inflation.

SPILLOVERS TO THE NONUNION SECTOR — UNION THREAT
But we have not yet examined the possibility that union-secured wage increases may spillover into the nonunion sector. Although the evidence is unsatisfactory, it is clear in principle that trade unions can influence the overall rate of wage inflation not merely by increasing union density and the union-nonunion differential but also by causing nonunion wages to rise at a faster rate than they would in the absence of unionism. An interesting hypothesis here is the so-called 'threat effect' of unionization. The argument is that union and nonunion wages are mutually interdependent. Thus union wages are positively related to those of the nonunion sector because the higher the nonunion wage the lower will be the employment cost to unions of an increase

in union wages, and conversely. But nonunion wages are also related positively with those of the union sector. A rising union-nonunion differential carries with it the increasing threat of unionization in the nonunion sector. Because employers believe that unionization raises production costs and reduces management flexibility, there will be a tendency for nonunion employers to raise their wage roles in tandem with union pay scales.

The attraction of the threat effect explanation is that it is a self-contained theory of wage inflation and relative income formation that, unlike other spillover theories, includes both unionized and nonunionized sectors of the labour market. Yet as Burton and Addison [11] have shown the dynamic predictions of the model closely resemble those of a market model once the union-nonunion differential attains its equilibrium value. In short, wage change is determined by excess demand and price expectations. However, unions can add an independent upthrust to the general rate of wage inflation if their preference for wage increases over the job security of their members becomes stronger. Attempts to apply the threat effect model have as usual resorted to ad hoc proxies in modelling this preference. [16]

The limited British empirical work in this area has concluded that, despite some 25 per cent of workers being covered by collective agreements without actually being union members, covered nonunion workers enjoy a modest (5 per cent) differential over uncovered nonunion workers. [42] The most recent U.S. evidence seems to suggest that, if anything, the union sector emulates the wage movements of the nonunion sector! [21] There is thus no strong evidence to suggest that the threat effect model provides a vehicle for the furnace analysis of the inflationary process.

MINIMUM WAGES AND SPILLOVERS

There remains the possibility that union wages spillover into nonunion wages via the operation of third party wage fixing machinery. Hard evidence of this effect is difficult to uncover for Britain. The evidence, such as it is does not suggest that wage council [17] minimum rates have kept pace with the *noncouncil* average since the 1940s. Thus the mean basic hourly wage rate in the wage council sector fell from around 86 per cent of the *noncouncil* average in 1950 to approximately 72 per cent in 1975. [52] However, the decline was by no means continuous, being concentrated in the post-1966 interval in which incomes policy norms were apparently more conscientiously applied in the wage council sector than elsewhere.

UNIONS GAIN AT EXPENSE OF OTHER WORKERS

Yet unions have supported the continuation of the wage council system, and presumably for reasons of self interest. Since union wage behaviour is not independent of wage rigidity elsewhere in the system we would argue that union support for wage councils has been to put a floor under competition. The most likely consequence of the resulting wage rigidity is an increase in the equilibrium or natural rate of unemployment. Unions thus redistribute income to themselves at the expense of the unorganized (i.e. lower paid workers).

D. SPILLOVERS IN THE PUBLIC SECTOR

Finally, we note the special problems confronting wage determination in public sector agencies. In the British case, comparison governs wage determination. The problem stems from the uncritical nature of the comparison exercise. In Britain, the most sophisticated mechanism for establishing rates of pay, by reference to levels of remuneration in outside employments, is the Civil Service Pay Research Unit (PRU). Since 1956, PRU has conducted regular pay surveys to establish the rates of pay of certain key grades in the civil service, linked to each of which are a plethora of subsidiary grades, termed 'consequentials,' whose pay rates are automatically adjusted in line with those of the key grades. The PRU 'master list' comprises most major employers in the private and public sectors who engage in collective bargaining with their white collar staffs. Initially, this series was based on *The Times* list of the top 500 British firms, and it appears to have remained relatively stable ever since. [20]

On a number of occasions during the early 1970s and the early 1980s the result of the comparison exercise led to large increases in pay for civil servants and indeed to their overtaking the private sector. The mechanisms producing these outcomes are less interesting than the more general problem of artificial comparability and will not be further discussed here. The real issue is the uncritical nature of the comparability process in the public sector underwritten by the absence of an ability to pay criterion. The basis of comparability is not static in the private sector. Rather, wage patterns evolve in line with changing labour and product market conditions. Wage patterns are not immutable and have a basis in economizing efforts and evolutionary processes. It is difficult to 'place' the public sector in the above framework. Reflecting this difficulty some observers have argued that the rates of pay for each occupation in the public sector should be determined by recruitment needs. [4] There are a number of difficulties with this solution, most obviously because establishment levels are themselves a subject of bargaining. The basic problem would seem to devolve on government readiness to play the part spender/lender of last resort to the British public sector, financing the public sector from general taxation and deficit finance (see section entitled "Unions as Fundamental Determinants of Inflation").

QUALIFICATIONS
The theoretical and statistical material surveyed above yields scant support for the argument that unions can influence wage change independently of market forces. Are we then to conclude that unions have little or no impact on the inflationary process? The causal links in the monetarist argument sketched in the introduction to this chapter might appear to lead us to this conclusion. But Friedman [22] himself specifically notes that unions may (a) lengthen the lags in the response of wage change to excess demand, (b) conceivably dampen the responsiveness of wage change to excess demand, or (c) even bias in an upward direction the rate of change of wages for a given level of demand. [18] (Point (c) goes some way toward the furnace view, except of course that the latter explicitly denies the role of demand.)

EVIDENCE ON THE COMPLETENESS OF THE MONETARIST EXPLANATION

What is the evidence on each of these qualifications to the monetarist analysis? The early literature provides a patchwork of conflicting evidence. Fortunately, the most recent literature provides a more uniform pattern of results.[19] It does appear that trade unions *inter al.* (see below) introduce long lags into wage change. Also, trade unions do seem to dampen the responsiveness of wage change to excess demand. There is little suggestion of inflationary bias, point (c), except at very low levels of inflation. On the other hand, unions apparently escalate wage reaction to price inflation. This latter finding is not explicable within the simple Friedmanite framework.

THE MULTI-PERIOD WAGE CONTRACT AND INFLATION

These results stem from modern analyses that seek explicitly to introduce labour market institutions into wage change analysis; and, in particular, multi-period wage contracts. When wages are set at discrete intervals as they are in practice, current wage changes will reflect conditions ruling at the time in the past when the contract was negotiated. Moreover, contracts reflect past changes in wages and prices in the interval between wage changes negotiated. As a result, the feedback response through lagged changes in wages and prices is central to the question of the magnitude and speed with which inflation responds to demand variables. In short, much of the short-run variation in inflation is due to the past history of excess demand and not current levels of excess demand. The wage inflation rate may thus act in a perverse fashion in the short-run — rising when unemployment is rising — depending on the structure of lags and the recent heritage of price inflation.

The dampening and escalating function of trade unions in terms of excess demand and price inflation respectively is a little more difficult to explain, not least because the suggestion is that trade unions are not themselves the real determining variable explaining differences between weakly organized and densely organized sectors.[20]

LONG-TERM CONTRACTS AND EMPLOYERS' INTERESTS

One reason for the existence of long-term contracts has to do with the nature of the employment relation. If firms have a long-term relation with much of the workforce (involving large doses of firm-specific training, for example) it makes sense to minimize transaction costs and institute procedures that encourage cooperation and information disclosure. Writing the contract for a number of years in advance, the payment of a wage premium, and the introduction of escalator clauses serve to increase the efficiency of internal labour market operation. The wage premium insulates the firm from day-to-day changes in labour market conditions while the presence of escalator or cost of living clauses promotes cooperation. In short, the long-term contract economizes on transaction costs.

LONG-TERM CONTRACTS AND UNIONS

Unfortunately, long-term contracts and wage premia are not simply reflective of the market situation described above. They also occur in oligopolistic and union situations. The problem, then, is to disentangle the independent contributions of each factor. The empirical studies on which we have earlier drawn do not establish the exogeneity or otherwise of trade unions. However, unionism is likely to be determined as well as determining. Until this lacuna is clarified we can only speculate on the independent impact of trade unions as a mediating influence through which more fundamental economic forces operate.

III. UNIONS AS FUNDAMENTAL DETERMINANTS OF INFLATION

We have seen that the evidence does not support the view that unions constitute a proximate or direct cause of inflation. That cause is instead to be located in the monetary sector. However, our discussion of union impact does not end here. Inflation arises directly because monetary expansion exceeds the growth in the supply of goods and services. Accordingly, unions may affect inflation by their impact on output growth or they may cause the money supply to expand faster than it would in their absence. Our knowledge of the sources of economic growth is too fragmentary to allow of a systematic test of union impact in the former area, although we shall subsequently provide evidence of unionism's productivity retarding role (Chapter Four). We can, however, say a little more about unionism's impact on the growth of the money supply. If unions do serve as a determinant of the growth rate of the money supply, they may be termed a fundamental cause of inflation.

Our understanding of the limited empirical research on the determinants of monetary growth is facilitated by a brief review of the spectrum of economists' views on the fundamental determinants of inflation.[21]

THE FUNDAMENTAL CAUSE OF INFLATION

The conventional monetarist argument à la Friedman [23] is eclectic on the causes of monetary expansion; it being argued that the forces leading governments to engage in inflationary finance have varied greatly from circumstance to circumstance with the result that it is impossible to point to the primacy of any one simple cause. For this reason it is not inconsistent with Friedman's own position to argue that union pressure on government may on occasion have led to expansion of the money supply. The main point, however, is that Friedman would deny the possibility that unions consistently act in this fashion. In short, unions are not a primary fundamental determinant of inflation.

UNIONS AS A DETERMINANT OF EXCESSIVE MONEY SUPPLY EXPANSION

Others who subscribe to the view that inflation is 'always and everywhere' a monetary phenomenon assign to unions a more than intermittent role in generating inflation. Thus Hayek [28] specifically indicts unions as a fundamental determinant. This arises because union wage pressures inflate the natural rate of unemployment. This action, taken in conjunction with government full employment policies, produces a cycle of inflation around a rising trend over the long term. The mechanism is as follows. A union induced increase in the equilibrium rate of unemployment leads governments to expand the budget deficit/money supply to reduce the rise in unemployment. This in turn alleviates considerably the constraints on union action in the economic marketplace (i.e. membership loss), leading once again to an increase in the natural unemployment rate. This cycle produces an acceleration in inflation through time.[22]

Why do governments behave in this self-defeating exercise? For Hayek, the answer is to be found in the slavish (and mistaken) pursuit of Keynesian full employment policies by postwar governments. It is not altogether clear, however, why governments do not learn. This remains an unsatisfactory element in the Hayekian treatment.

It is also a conspicuous lacuna of the standard cost-push argument. Kahn, [36] for example, similarly emphasizes the commitment of postwar governments to full employment policies; a commitment that often takes the form of a specific target rate of unemployment. To this extent, certain cost-push analysts appear to accept that this commitment rather than autonomous 'wage push' is the fundamental determinant of inflation. Union-induced jumps in the rate of inflation (the proximate cause) leave the authorities with no option other than to accommodate. The price is an increase in inflation.

In an innovative analysis, Gordon [26] attempts to demystify the role of government in the above treatments. Gordon presents an analysis of the demand for and supply of inflation. On the demand side, Gordon examines the potential gains for different groups that flow from inflationary policies. Such groups are seen as having a 'demand' for inflation. This pressure, manifested via voting and lobbying, is an implicit rather than explicit demand for inflation. On the supply side, governments are depicted as vote-maximizing agencies, seeking the electoral profit from the manipulation of fiscal and monetary policies. Bringing both sides together, Gordon contends that inflation is the vote maximizing response of government to the direct and indirect pressures exerted by potential beneficiaries of inflation. Union members are seen as the principal beneficiaries and for this reason are diagnosed as a primary fundamental determinant of inflation.

Interestingly, Gordon emphasizes the role of unions in the economic marketplace in identifying them as a fundamental determinant of inflation. The source of the gain to union members is wage push which, when accommodated for vote maximizing reasons, redistributes income in their favour. This mechanism is however flawed. What is the incentive for unions to push if, as Gordon's own detailed analysis suggests, the gains from inflation are but transitory? That is to say, once we introduce all the relevant long-run considerations into the Gordon model, the incentive for unions to push *continuously* through time simply evaporates.[23]

Burton [9] has argued that although the rationality of wage push is not evident at the macro level it may nonetheless be rational at the union level on the grounds that if one union does not push then another will! However, this argument for wage push is eroded by our earlier analysis of proximate causation *and* Burton's reflections elsewhere in this volume (Chapter One) noting the limited scope for redistribution in the economic marketplace. The discussion thus shifts to the public expenditure route. Inflationary finance remains an attractive instrument of redistribution toward themselves for powerful political groups, including unions.

EVIDENCE ON THE POLITICAL ECONOMY OF INFLATION

With these preliminaries behind us, what of the empirical evidence with a bearing on the issues. Unfortunately, research into the 'political economy' of inflation is in its infancy. The literature is sparse and has to be interpreted with extreme caution. Thus Willett and Laney, [57] for example, find that both wage inflation and the budget deficit are important determinants of British (and Italian) monetary growth. Yet the authors acknowledge that their analysis does not firmly establish the linkages to the money supply, so that the direction of causation may run from money supply to wages rather than the converse. There is also controversy as to the role of the budget deficit. The conventional argument is that government borrowing from the public is noninflationary provided that increasing public deficits do not adversely affect price expectations. However, Minford [41] has recently argued that monetary policy cannot be systematically independent of the budget deficit.[24]

Unfortunately, as we shall see, the contribution of the deficit to monetary growth is less than transparent in the empirical literature.

The major study on which we can draw is that of Gordon, [27] who examines the determinants of monetary growth (*inter al.*) for an eight-country sample covering two periods 1958-1973 and 1958-1978. Gordon plays closer attention than do Willett and Laney to the direction of causation issue. He uses a fairly well known, albeit controversial, statistical procedure to establish whether the money supply is truly independent of wage pressures or is instead determined by them.[25]

Looking first at his money supply findings, Gordon detects no evidence from his total sample that wage rate movements determine the rate of growth of the money supply. Only for the United States is there any evidence of feedback from wages to the money supply. Yet this passive accommodation occurs in the very country in which, according to this study, there is no sign of autonomous wage push.

Turning to wage behaviour, Gordon finds that the growth of the money supply significantly affects wage change for the total sample and for a number of individual countries including, most interestingly, the United Kingdom where the influence of money supply growth on wages is stronger than for any other country in the sample! A basic feature of the statistical tests, however, is the procedure used to identify intervals of (autonomous) wage push. Since the average impact of wage push intervals is determined by 'peeking at the data' it is not surprising that subsequent analysis yields evidence of wage push.

As for price change, wage push emerges as a generally insignificant factor in inflation. Only for the United Kingdom is there any evidence of significant effect. The small estimated effect of money on prices is notable, but as pointed out by Parkin [45] the author's use of *domestic* money supply calls into question the specification of the wage and price change relationship.

This then is a fairly mixed bag of results giving little strong support to any simple relationship explaining either inflation or changes in the money supply. If anything,

Gordon's results favour the (international) monetarist argument rather than his preferred model. [26] This is perhaps not an unexpected result but it has only the most limited bearing on a political economy model of inflation. In a very real sense Gordon's empirical analysis returns us to the question with which we started out; namely, what determines the growth rate of the money supply. If, as Gordon's results seem to testify, the monetary authorities in various countries behave in different fashion then the task is to explain this diversity.

POLITICAL GAMES AND THE MONEY SUPPLY

It was earlier argued by Burton (Chapter One) that the 'game' being played in the political marketplace is too complicated to allow for any simple explanation. We should not therefore expect to find a clear econometric relationship between union influence in the political market and inflation. This is also the burden of Gordon's [26] theoretical analysis of the demand for and supply of inflation, although his statistical analysis shows no such concern for these subtleties.

Unfortunately, only limited progress has been made in applying the insights from public choice theory† to variables relevant to a discussion of the fundamental determinants of inflation. Conventional economic analysis has for its part failed to detect a robust association between, say, the size of the budget deficit and inflation, or between public spending and inflation. Thus Gordon [27] fails to detect evidence of monetarization of fiscal deficits — only in the case of Japan is there a significant positive relation between the size of the deficit and the rate of growth of the money supply. Similarly, Peacock and Ricketts [46] fail to find a strong link between inflation and (a) the tax share of GNP, (b) the public expenditure share of GNP, and (c) public sector growth. Interestingly, the authors acknowledge that their negative results are "not altogether surprising given that the simple hypotheses concerning the size and growth of the public sector are so tenuously related to public choice theory." [45]

---

†Editor's note: Public choice theory is an analysis of politics using the tools of economics.

However, some progress has been made in analyzing the demand side determinants of public spending, using a choice theoretic approach. Thus Dudley and Montmarquette, [16] in analyzing nonmilitary public spending across a sample of 52 countries, test whether that spending is determined by the actions of the median voter or, as is more consistent with the arguments developed in this monograph, by a specific interest group. The specific interest in question is the government bureaucracy. According to the so-called leviathan model, [6] state bureaucracies come to play an important role in the legislative process (i.e. distort voter choices) by which their budgets are determined with a resulting increase in the public share. Moreover, as the public sector grows, it is argued that the direct political power of public employees expressed in the ballot box will lead to further increases in both public sector employment and wages.

Dudley and Montmarquette find that the leviathan model has stronger empirical credentials than the alternative median voter model. The authors also detect that a higher mean wage, *for a given level of per capita income*, is associated with higher levels of public expenditure. This result they interpret as reflecting intercountry differences in the preference for public expenditure. More narrowly, they argue that the higher is the wage level the more likely there are to be distortions in the labour market. With wage rates above competitive levels there will be a demand for increased public spending to create jobs and to transfer essential services and purchasing power to those who risk unemployment. This uncertainty argument is not tested directly and may be consistent with the crude association between trade unions and public expenditure. [12]

The role of the government bureaucracy is also emphasized in Borjas' [5] excellent study of wage determination within the agencies of the U.S. government. In this model, government is perceived as a vote maximizing institution, purchasing political support by the redistributing of State revenues to politically powerful interest groups. The federal bureaucracy can alternatively hinder or facilitate this redistributive process and thus indirectly influence the amount of political support, as well as directly influencing that support through its own voting behaviour as in the leviathan model. Thus the government seeks to maximize its total political support by redistributing its resources optimally among competing interest groups subject to its budget[26] and the actions of bureaucrats who may be expected to hinder the flow of agency 'output' when their wage is low and increase it when their wage is high. Borjas is able to find strong empirical confirmation regarding his hypotheses that agency salaries will be directly related to the power of bureaucrats to control output and to the political organization of the agency's constituency.

This benefit-constraint analysis, while leaving a number of important questions unanswered, provides an appropriate framework for analyzing the impct of 'organized' labour on public expenditure. The ultimate aim is to formulate and test a full political economy model of inflation. The basic building blocks of this inquiry involve the determination of the 'optimal' amount of public expenditure, analysis of the manner in which this expenditure is financed, and investigation of the interaction between budget and the central bank.

In the interim, our prejudice that unions are indeed a fundamental determinant of inflation is qualified by the lack of empirical evidence that points directly to that outcome. The evidence surveyed here is suggestive rather than definitive on the role of unions as a fundamental determinant of inflation.

IV. CONCLUSIONS

In the light of the foregoing, it is apparent that unionism's role in the inflationary process is somewhat clouded. We can be fairly certain that unions have not been a primary proximate cause of inflation, except perhaps in periods of very low inflation rates. Unions and other labour market institutions do appear profoundly to affect the mechanism of the inflationary process for reasons related to the timing of discrete wage and price changes. We are presently unable to disentangle the particular contribution of unionism per se to the inflation problem seen in terms of complex lag structures. This is one area where union impact (as a mechanism or mediating institution through which market forces operate) is clouded, though this does not disturb the general conclusion that unions are not a direct cause of inflation.

One way of summarizing union impact on inflation at the proximate level is to exploit the simple identity that changes in the average wage level reflect movements in the nonunion wage, changes in union density and changes in the union-nonunion differential. On the basis of this simple identity, union influence via the two latter channels contributed only 10 per cent to a total U.K. wage inflation of 170 per cent over the period 1961-1965. [44] We cite this result for emphasis without attributing behavioural content to the identity.

Having exonerated trade unions as a proximate determinant of inflation, we would nonetheless indict them as a fundamental determinant, along with other special interest groups. Such groups have an implicit demand for inflation which vote maximizing governments accommodate via the inflation tax. Yet we are at present far from being able to quantify the impact of trade unions in this area. Developments within public choice theory promise to assist in this ultimate aim. In the interim, we have merely assembled fragments of empirical information that are consistent with our interpretation of unionism's role, while seeking to chart a positive research agenda.

CHAPTER THREE

UNIONISM, PRODUCTIVITY AND GROWTH

John T. Addison

I. INTRODUCTION

The role of trade unions in inhibiting growth and contributing to low levels of efficiency — the third symptom of the British disease — is a controversial topic of enquiry. Recently, the controversy has deepened with the emergence of a provocative *American* research literature that has purported to show that unionism actually increases productivity. Economists associated with what I have chosen to term the 'Harvard School,' [2] by substituting systematic study for casual empiricism and anecdotal evidence, have challenged the orthodox view that unions impact adversely on productivity. Given this important new empirical literature, part of our discussion will be given over to the new view of unionism. This discussion is appropriate in the context of the British disease because it will enable us to present a developing theme while facilitating a comparison of the British and North American experiences.

In the following we first consider some facts of British productivity and economic growth. Next, we address the important Harvard literature. We then discuss why the quantitative impact of collective bargaining on productivity may be greater in Britain than in North America. Finally, we question how uniquely British a symptom is this facet of the British disease.

II. BRITAIN'S RELATIVE PRODUCTIVITY AND GROWTH RECORD

A LONG-STANDING PROBLEM

The first observation to make is that there is nothing particularly new in Britain's sluggish productivity and growth performance. As early as 1907, for example, physical product per person employed in representative British manufacturing industries was on average no more than one-half that of their U.S. counterparts; [35] while Maddison's [27] data suggest that between 1870 and 1976 the average level of output per head in sixteen industrial countries rose six-fold compared with only a four-fold rise in the U.K. In consequence of this cumulative development, most EEC countries had by the end of this period levels of GDP per capita at purchasing power exchange rates that exceeded by some 30 to 40 per cent the British level.

We noted above that as early as 1907 physical product per employee in British manufacturing was only one-half the corresponding U.S. value. A productivity shortfall of the same order of magnitude was reported by Rostas [39] in a more systematic study of labour productivity differences between the two countries. Rostas' findings were broadly confirmed by the productivity teams formed by the Anglo-American Council on Productivity, which made comparisons across a wide range of trades. A subsequent study by Ray [36] of productivity in plants of comparable size in Britain and Germany found that output per head was between 4 and 29 per cent higher in Germany in the printing industry, between 6 and 27 per cent higher in chemicals, and up to 20 per cent higher in shipbuilding. Similar findings were reported by the tripartite National Economic Development Office (NEDO) in a number of sponsored studies in the 1960s and 1970s: one such study of the chemical industry reporting that output per employee in the U.S. was up to 85 per cent in excess of British productivity after allowing for differences in the scale of production. [30] Invidious comparisons between productivity levels in the U.K. and the U.S. have also been drawn for the steel and oil refining industries. [6] [18]1

ISOLATING THE ROLE OF UNIONS

Needless to say, it has proved difficult to separate the contribution of collective bargaining to the British deficit in productivity — let alone growth — from the effects of differences in product mix and quality, scale of production, capital vintage and the like. While the above studies point to marked residual differences between Britain and her industrial market economy counterparts, their controls are rudimentary and they fail to quantify the contributions of the cause of productivity differences.

INTERNATIONAL COMPARISONS OF UNION EFFECTS ON PRODUCTIVITY

A recent comparative study by Pratten [34] has made perhaps the best attempt to date to come to grips with these problems. Specifically, Pratten compared labour productivity at the British and the overseas factories of international companies in which absolute levels of labour productivity might be expected to be more comparable because of similarities in product and technology. Pratten collected comparisons from 100 companies and calculated the following (unweighted) averages for the percentage differentials between ten other industrial countries and Britain: United States and Canada, +50 per cent; West Germany, +27 per cent; Italy, +16 per cent; France, +15 per cent; Sweden and Denmark, +22 per cent; Spain, -11 per cent; Australia and New Zealand, -15 per cent; Brazil, -15 per cent. (Of the differences shown, only those for the United States and Canada, West Germany and France are statistically significant.)

Pratten also sought to assess the contribution of economic and 'behavioural' factors (e.g. strikes, restrictive practices, and overmanning) to the overall productivity differential (where that was statistically significant). A summary of his results is given in Table 3.1, from which it can be seen that labour relations contributed roughly one-quarter of the United Kingdom's short-fall relative to the U.S. and Canada, one-third of that relative to France, and one-half of that relative to Germany.

Table 3.1
Estimates of the Causes of Productivity[a] Differentials between the U.K., North America, France, and Germany

Cause	Country Comparison		
	U.K./ Germany	U.K./ France	U.K./ N. America
Economic			
Differences in scale of output and length of production run	5½	1½	20½
Differences in plant and machinery	5	5	(6)
Other[b]	(2)	(2)	(6)
Total	(13)	(9)	(35)
'Behavioural'			
Strikes and major restrictive practices	3½	0	5
Other[c]	(8½)	(5½)	(6)
Total	(12)	(5½)	(11)
Average Differential	27	15	50

Note: The contributions to the productivity differentials are multiplicative, not additive.

(a) The figures in parenthesis indicate possible orders of magnitude.

(b) Other economic causes include differences in product mix, the substitution of labour for materials, capacity utilization, and the availability of labour.

(c) Other behavioural causes comprise differences in manning and efficiency.

Source: C.F. Pratten (1976), *Labour Productivity Differences within International Companies*, Cambridge: Cambridge University Press, Table 9.1, p. 61.

We have some insight from this study into the possible orders of magnitude involved, although problems of selectivity bias likely attach to Pratten's estimates.[2] Note, however, that one cannot attribute all of the 'behavioural' effects to the labour force, not least because feather-bedding and other practices imply some form of management complicity. That fact notwithstanding we can fairly safely conclude that labour practices themselves are of importance in causing departures from the most efficient use of capital and labour.

The most recent study of Britain's productivity shortfall is Caves' [10] comparison of factor productivity in 71 British and American manufacturing industries. Caves reports that the quality of management inputs, plant size and work stoppages are all negatively correlated in Britain with relative industrial productivity.

Caves' statistical analysis shows that the ratio of productivity in British manufacturing industries to productivity in U.S. industries is negatively correlated with strikes in British industries. Moreover, Caves reports that the ratio of British inventory-to-sales figures to those for U.S. industries are positively correlated with variables representing the state of labour relations in British industries. This particular finding is of course *prima facie* consistent with the familiar argument that the large number of short, unofficial strikes in Britain creates much uncertainty in the planning of output.

His principal finding in terms of statistical significance is, however, that British productivity is lower in industries requiring technical and managerial skills. In other words, deficient British management may be the chief villain in the piece. We note in passing that Caves found that size of plant is not a significant determinant of poor productivity performance.

Unfortunately, Caves' study is subject to a number of statistical and other difficulties that are so serious as to call into question its findings.[3] His focus on managerial deficiencies is, however, at once relevant and controversial. Clearly, much fuller investigation of the role of the quality of management is required, especially in the light of the recent American studies reviewed in the next section.

Finally, we need to make the point that in assessing the impact of collective bargaining on productivity one should first look to differences between union and nonunion plants. It is to a discussion of these differences that we next turn.

III. PRODUCTIVITY IN THE UNION AND NONUNION SECTORS

A. TWO VIEWS OF THE EFFECTS OF UNIONS ON PRODUCTIVITY

THE USUAL VIEW

The orthodox view of trade unions is that they are monopolies that impose allocative costs via their distortion of the wage structure while also generating nonwage induced inefficiencies via their job regulatory practices. North American studies [4] point to fairly modest output losses from the former channel. Thus, for the U.S., Rees. [37] has computed the output loss at $600 million in a $443 billion economy (the U.S. in 1957). In this computation he assumes a union-nonunion wage differential of 15 per cent and that the demand for labour in the union and nonunion sector rises and falls by the same percentage as wages. However, Burton [9] arrives at a considerably higher estimate of the output loss for Britain, namely 3 per cent of national output as compared with Rees' 0.14 per cent. Since both authors use the same methods to calculate the output loss effect, the different values simply reflect different assumptions as to the union-nonunion differential (40 per cent in Burton's study) and objective differences in the size of the unionized labour force in the two countries.

Turning to nonwage induced inefficiencies, Rees *guesses* that these are at least equal to the wage effects. He arrives at an overall value of unionism's direct and indirect output loss effects of somewhat under 1 per cent of national output. Similarly, Burton simply doubles his estimate of the indirect output loss effect to yield a total output loss of about 6 per cent of national output.

While we would caution that Burton's estimates are somewhat on the high side,[5] we would also note that the assumptions made in calculating output loss effects understate the orders of magnitude involved. First, the estimates assume that labour shed from the union sector is able without friction to find employment in the nonunion sector. Second, the implicit assumption made in such calculations is that the additional earnings received by union members represent a costless transfer of purchasing power extracted from the rest of the economy. Since neither assumption holds in reality, the above estimates, if otherwise acceptable, will represent lower bound estimates of unionism's true output loss effects, other things being equal.

THE NEW VIEW
Yet it has been argued recently that other things are not equal; that the direct output effects of unionism are positive rather than negative and may even outweigh the indirect output effects resulting from union distortion of the wage structure. Importantly, this argument is based on systematic empirical enquiry, whereas studies prior to the Harvard analyses, although consistent with the predictions of the orthodox economic theory, either had a basis in casual empiricism or were simply ad hoc. In short, until the Harvard studies burst on the scene there was little in the way of systematic evidence to support orthodoxy. By stepping into this empirical void, the new research literature to some extent undermined orthodoxy. Yet, as we shall subsequently argue, the Harvard findings have to be taken with more than a pinch of statistical salt. Meanwhile, let us consider the theory behind the new view of unions.

The basic theory underpinning the Harvard studies is articulated by Freeman [20] and, to a lesser extent, by Freeman and Medoff. [21] Unions can, so the argument runs, enhance productivity because they serve as a vehicle for expressing the collective view of workers. The importance of having such a vehicle arises from the fact that uniform company policy and shared working conditions will inevitably imply restrictions on individual behaviour and imperfect matching of preferences. Also, work effort is often a shared responsibility requiring collective adherence to a work plan and minimization of shirking. [6]

BENEFITS OF COLLECTIVE ACTION
In this situation, there are fairly obvious benefits attaching to collective action. First, unions can act as a source of information regarding employee needs and preferences and can assist in the evaluation of complex wage and benefit offers. Without some form of collective organization, preference revelation would be under provided. This is a simple agency function of collective organization but is taken to be synonymous with autonomous unions by both Freeman and by Freeman and Medoff. Second, there is also a governance function of unions and it is presumably here that the principal supposed benefits of collective voice lie, since the agency role is little more than an instrumental one that permits the parties to reach preferred bargains. This voice component is the political side of unionism. Its efficiency properties have a basis in the continuity needs of the parties. Thus Freeman writes:

> Because of on-the-job skills specific to enterprises. . . . and the cost of mobility and turnover, there are gains to be had from regular employment, a continuing relation between firms and much of their work force, in which allocative and remunerative decisions are not directly controlled by the market mechanism.[7]

Thus it would seem that the gains from collective voice stem from reducing bargaining costs, rationalizing the work structure, encouraging cooperation of a substantive rather than perfunctory nature, and encouraging investments by the firm in the worker and by the worker in the firm without the risk of exploitation by either side. These elements are not spelled out by Freeman, but presumably constitute the kernel of productivity enhancement.

SHOCK EFFECTS OF UNIONIZATION
Neither Freeman nor Freeman and Medoff discount the existence of a pronounced 'shock effect' attendant upon unionization, although this is an essentially indirect source of productivity improvement stemming from the wage differential (higher wages shock inefficient management into adopting more efficient methods of production). The shock effect may thus be said to represent a much attenuated form of the collective voice model.

To sum up: it is argued that the public goods dimension of the workplace calls for collective action, which is taken to be synonymous with autonomous unionism. By providing a means of expressing discontent beyond exiting/quitting, collective voice is said to reduce quits and absenteeism. Voice also produces an institutional mechanism for innovation in labour contracts. Finally, managements may simply be shocked into improving production methods by having to pay higher wages. Apart from the quits mechanism, the sources of productivity enhancement are not clearly articulated.

DIFFICULTIES WITH THE NEW VIEW
There are a number of difficulties with the Harvard model. First, and most obvious, the net effect of the introduction of unions is ambiguous. Freeman, [20] for example, cautions that the gains from collective voice depend on the response of management to collective bargaining and the response of unions to reorganization of the workplace. Second, it is not altogether clear whether Freeman and Medoff [21] view the economic system as pervasively inefficient to begin with, or as responding in a cost minimizing way to the problems of incomplete information that they correctly identify as typifying *certain* exchange relationships. In the former case, there is little assurance that union action will improve the situation, while in the latter it is hard to perceive of unions as a truly exogenous or independent variable. (We shall return to these points below.) Third, no specific theory of union behaviour is offered.

THE STATISTICAL EVIDENCE
Turning to the empirical evidence, data purporting to identify a positive union effect on productivity have been supplied in six studies: Allen, 1979; Brown and Medoff, 1978; Clark, 1980a,b; Frantz, 1976; Freeman, Medoff and Connerton, 1982. All six studies employ a production function approach, in which output per unit of labour is depicted as depending on the capital-labour ratio and union density *inter al.* [8] The union density variable is used to capture the change in output attributable to unionism. Union labour may appear more 'productive' as management responds to

the higher union wage by substituting capital for labour and/or by substituting higher for lower quality workers. It is therefore necessary to isolate these spurious union productivity effects. The first effect is neutralized by holding the amount of capital per worker constant by including it in the production function. Worker 'quality' is held constant by measuring labour in such a way that more qualified workers represent more labour units.

Only in the case of one study (and here for only one of the sample periods under investigation) is a negative union productivity effect reported. Otherwise, positive effects, that in most cases either equal or exceed the union relative wage gain, are measured. This has led the Harvard analysts to conclude that unionized firms can after all compete with their unorganized counterparts in otherwise regular markets.

CHALLENGING CONVENTIONAL WISDOM?
Given their substitution of systematic study for casual empiricism, one effect of these studies has been to throw into the melting pot the conventional, static analysis of unionism. Another has been to convince the hitherto agnostic that the economic effect of unions is, after all, benign.

FOUR SERIOUS FLAWS IN HARVARD STUDIES
In fact, the various Harvard studies are more or less seriously flawed. A few brief comments will here suffice to establish the basic lines of criticism.[9]

First, the studies by Clark, [12] [13] which remedy a number of major statistical difficulties associated with the other studies,[10] yield fairly unimpressive results. Thus, closer inspection of the statistical significance of the unionism variable in Clark's [13] major cross-section study of 128 unionized and nonunionized plants leads to the conclusion that he has only demonstrated that trade unions have no effect one way or the other on productivity.[11] (This is at odds with Clark's own interpretation of his findings.) His smaller, longitudinal study of six plants that changed union status (from nonunion to union) in the sample period 1953-1976 is perhaps the stronger analytical study, but the test procedure is asymmetric in that no account is taken of those plants that changed union status in an opposite direction. Also, the sample size is sufficiently small, and the correction for time trends sufficiently crude to cast reasonable doubt on the reliability of the author's estimates.

Second, the various studies fail conspicuously to identify the sources of productivity improvement, and have simply focused on net effects.[12] The bottom line is apparently that unions 'cause' higher productivity by shocking management into more efficient production methods. Unfortunately, the shock effect model lacks dynamic content. Thus, are we to assume that repeated shocks will lead to continued increases in productivity? (See section on "The Role of the Collective Bargaining System.") While a similar accusation can be levelled at the orthodox theory, this can after all be supplemented by human capital theoretic considerations which would emphasize the job *protective* nature of many union working practices.

Third, the collective voice model strictly interpreted would appear to apply only to industrial-type labour markets. This point is conceded by Freeman[13] although this caveat appears to have been forgotten in other Harvard renditions of the collective voice parable. We should not be surprised to learn that industrial-type labour markets offer the least fertile setting for the generation of nonwage, union-induced inefficiencies, at least in the private sector. Here, too, unionism will intrude upon a 'natural' seniority system predicated on profit maximization.

Fourth, it is nowhere established that collective voice requires autonomous unions. Even if it does, there are other troublesome issues to consider. For example, to what extent is the collective voice provided by unions muffled by policy concerns of the national union leadership? Again, there is the fundamental problem of causality because unionism may be a response to 'unfavourable' (i.e. structured, inflexible and fast paced hence, productive) working conditions. Therefore the productivy differential observed as well as the presence of the union may jointly arise from the nature of the workplace.[14]

The scope of these criticisms is such as to call into serious question the findings of the Harvard School analysts. Also, there are other pieces of empirical evidence that contest the unions-raise-productivity thesis.

CONTRADICTORY EVIDENCE FROM THE U.K.

Curiously enough, the Harvard studies were anticipated by an excellent British study that reported a very different set of findings. Pencavel [33] analyzed the relative performance of the unionized sector of the British coal mining industry, 1900-1913. First of all, Pencavel provides evidence that the unions did not create a wage differential. Accordingly his analysis is not contaminated by the wage effects mentioned above.[15] Next, Pencavel tests the hypothesis that unionized coalfields are uniformly less productive than nonunion coalfields. Formally, he tests whether the efficiency para-meter of the production function — i.e. the ability to get output from a given amount of input — varies inversely with unionization. The efficiency parameter is also assumed to vary with time and the mean width of coal seams (to take account of the geological elements in coal production).

Pencavel tests two specifications of the union effect. The first examines the relationship between proportionate changes in output and the proportionate change in union density. The second relates the proportionate change in output to changes in the level of organization. Pencavel's first test indicated that a 10 per cent increase in the fraction of the workforce unionized reduced productivity by 1.1 per cent. Given that the fraction unionized in coal mining rose from 66 per cent to 80 per cent over the period in question, it may be inferred that this development was associated with a reduction in coal output of 2.3 per cent (-0.110 x 21.2 per cent).

The formulation which assumed that the reduction in output is related to the level of organization was also not rejected by the data and indicates a depressing effect of unions on productivity of 3.1 per cent. Taking this latter value, production of coal at the end of the sample period would have been 9 million tons above its actual level had the fraction of miners unionized remained at its 1900 value. Indeed, extending his results beyond the range of sample observations, yields the conclusion that a totally unionized coalfield would produce some 22 per cent less output than its completely unorganized counterpart. Pencavel's findings provide some support for the assertions made at that time that the growth of unionism did contribute to the declining productivity of British coal mining because of increased absenteeism, a rising disputes trend, a cut in hours, *plus* the reduced fear on the part of miners of the disciplinary actions of employers in the wake of unionization.

CONTRADICTORY EVIDENCE FROM THE U.S.

Interestingly, the most recent U.S. literature also pours cold water on both the generality and substance of the unions-raise-productivity thesis. The literature dealing with economic growth will be reviewed in the section on "How British is the British Disease?" Here we simply focus on a recent study by Clark [14] which confirms our suspicion that unionism's effect on resource allocation is essentially a question about the long-run.

UNION EFFECTS ON PRODUCTIVITY — A WIDER SAMPLE

In his analysis of 900 'product line' businesses in the U.S., 1970-1980, Clark first detects that the impact of unionism on productivity is consistently negative, although not always significantly so. Second, and potentially much more important, unionism is found to exert a significantly negative effect on profits of around 19 per cent relative to the sample mean. This effect appears furthermore to be strongly dependent on market structure.

UNIONS HURT COMPETITIVE FIRMS MORE

When the firm sample is broken up into low market share (less than 10 per cent) and high market share (over 35 per cent) firms, unionism reduces profits in the former by close to 40 per cent while in the latter the effect is insignificant. While this result requires further scrutiny it carries important implications for the impact of unions on productivity in the long run. A disproportionate effect of unionism on competitive firms threatens the survival of such firms and may well constitute an added barrier to entry. Unionism may, then, intrude upon the competitive dynamics of an industry and influence market structure. There is clearly a pressing need for further studies in this area. Meanwhile, we have an additional explanation of why unionized firms may survive over long periods of time that is directly at odds with the standard Harvard School explanation: unionized and nonunionized firms are not after all competing in otherwise regular markets.

We note that Clark's study, human capital considerations (investment in skills), and the political dimension of union power all lead in the same direction in suggesting that unionism's effect on resource allocation is really a question of the long run. The static consequences of unionism may indeed be fairly small but we can be less sanguine as to its effect in the long-run. The growth literature reviewed below appears to bear this out.

B. EVIDENCE ON THE PRODUCTIVITY REDUCING EFFECTS OF UNIONS IN THE U.K.

The organizational features of British unionism (see the following section) are such as to suggest that its static consequences may be more serious than is the case in North America. The almost uniquely British flirtation with 'productivity bargaining' provides some indication of the intra-firm allocative inefficiencies and other lapses from efficiency associated with British unionism. A snag in interpreting this data is that plants engaging in productivity bargaining were almost exclusively unionized prior to the exercise. As noted earlier, a systematic test should seek to compare unionized with nonunionized establishments. Also, the artificial grafting of productivity bargaining on to incomes policy (as an allowed exception to wage norms and ceilings) led to bogus or 'phoney' agreements. Be this as it may, productivity bargaining held out some promise for eliminating restrictive/protective practices precisely because it offered workers a *quid pro quo* in return for the abandonment of such practices. The increase in productivity arising from these agreements provides some indication of the on-going effects of restrictive/protective practices.

BUYING OUT OF LOW PRODUCTIVITY

Major increases in productivity were reported in a number of well publicized productivity agreements; perhaps the best known of which was concluded in 1960 at the Fawley refinery of Standard Oil of New Jersey. This agreement was prompted by the discovery that the Fawley refinery had considerably higher unit costs than its U.S. counterparts using similar technology. The so-called 'Blue Book' agreement at Fawley yielded increases of 40 per cent in hourly rates of pay, spread over two years, in return for relaxation of job demarcations, withdrawal of craftsmen's mates (see below) and their redeployment on other work, additional temporary and permanent shift working, and greater freedom in the use of supervision. Over the two year life of the agreement, output per man hour rose by approximately 50 per cent and refinery overtime was reduced to 7.5 per cent (from 18 per cent of total hours worked) as average working time declined by 5½ hours. Although less progress was achieved on *intercraft* flexibility — only 5 per cent of craftsmen's time after the agreement was found to be spent working outside the craft — craftsmen's mates were eliminated and substantial flexibility was achieved among process workers. Major improvements in productivity were also recorded elsewhere, at least in the early agreements negotiated during the first half of the 1960s. Estimated net reductions in the neighborhood of 10 to 15 per cent of the wage bill were not uncommon.

INCOMES POLICY SPOILS THE OPTION
Unfortunately, productivity bargaining fell into disrepute toward the end of the 1960s. Between January 1967 and December 1969 some 4,185 (private sector) productivity cases were reported to the vetting agency (Department of Employment and Productivity), compared with a total of only 73 agreements over 1963-1966. By 1969 some 8.2 million workers, or 36 per cent of employees in employment, were covered by productivity or analogous agreements. Many observers were alarmed by the scale of this development given the stringency of the productivity guidelines set down by the incomes policy agency, the National Board for Prices and Incomes (although the vetting agency within the Department of Employment was little more than a man and a dog operation). The national figures for production and man-hours showed little evidence of a sharp rise in labour productivity and what favourable trends were dis-

cernible were attributed by many to other factors such as the recession-induced shake-out of labour in the latter half of the 1960s. Rising levels of unemployment, meantime, weakened labour's commitment to the new bargaining instrument, even where explicit 'no redundancy' clauses were featured in agreements.

It soon became clear, to state the obvious, that many productivity agreements were indeed fraudulent and intended solely to avoid the strictures of wage control policy. Moreover, the high straight-time hourly wage gains necessary to 'buy' genuine productivity gain would appear to have had a wage demonstration effect for other workers.[17] Both developments were affected by incomes policy and both threatened the continuation of the buy-out principle in follow-up or second generation agreements. For these and other reasons, wide-scale productivity bargaining did not long survive the pervasive incomes policy experimentation of the 1960s.

PRODUCTIVITY BUY OUT — A SOUND PRINCIPLE?
Yet excessive revulsion against the basic approach (and its further development in the form of 'efficiency bargaining') is as misguided as the initial rapturous reception given to the offset agreement by many so-called industrial relations experts. There is manifestly no single cure-all that will remedy every conceivable illness from industrial malnutrition to manpower and wage bill obesity. [38] But this is not to imply that the correct medicine taken in the appropriate circumstances cannot cause some cures. A prime candidate for the application of the surgical techniques of productivity bargaining (or for efficiency audits) is the public sector.

PRODUCTIVITY IN THE PUBLIC SECTOR
The public/nationalized sector may on theoretical grounds be expected to provide the clearest examples of organizational slack and featherbedding. As a case in point one might cite British Rail. This agency currently has a surplus staff in the region of 38,000 — a figure accepted by a 1977 Commons select committee and by British Rail itself. This surplus complement adds 300 million pounds or so to the wages bill. At the time of writing, it appears that 80 per cent

of locomotives and high speed trains are double manned, a practice that ceased on most other European railways systems a decade ago. Also contrary to European practice, British Rail continues to operate freight trains with guards. Again, the Associated Society of Locomotive Engineers and Firemen insist that one set of drivers deal with Southern electric commuter trains while other drivers are consigned to freight only. This inevitably implies down time for commuter drivers outside the peak. As a consequence of these and analogous practices, manning levels in British Rail are quite clearly out of line with Scandinavian, French and German railways. British Rail, meanwhile, is sustained by a subsidy of 3 million pounds a day, which indicates at least a passive management complicity in the arrangement.

A GENERALIZED BUY-OUT OF UNION 'BADS'?

Some have advocated buying out all the collective 'bads' associated with unionism, not merely those stemming from the rule book. Having diagnosed unions as a collective bad from the viewpoint of society as a whole, Burton [9] advocates this very solution. He argues that the attempt to remove monopolistic distortions poses a genuine free rider problem. If there were some means of reaching and policing such an agreement, it would clearly benefit all consumers to join to provide a lump sum payment to trade unions equal to their various monopoly gains in return for the abandonment of their monopolistic distortions. But the costs of this collective activity and of policing the resulting 'contract' are positive. Unfortunately, the removal of the public bad once accomplished, would be available to all whether they had helped bear the costs of removal or not. Private collective action would thus seem unable to achieve an optimal removal of monopoly distortion, and hence the case made on public goods grounds for State intervention to restore competitive pricing in the labour market. Burton proposes that the lump-sum buy-out be financed by the issue of long-term public debt; thereafter permitting company-wide though not connective or industry-wide bargaining and possibly subjecting unions to antitrust legislation analogous to that employed in product markets. Whatever the practicability of this particular suggestion, a case can be made for using buy-out in piecemeal fashion to attack such problems as the closed shop and, of course, intraplant inefficiencies. In this latter context, buy-out is a surgical operation conducted at discrete intervals. Apart from the obvious problem that compensation might encourage a further development of inefficient working arrangements by putting a premium on inefficiency, there is the related point that the instrument is a fairly blunt method of dealing with the technological change that is often the occasion for productivity reducing work rules. While productivity bargaining has in some plants evolved and taken on the formal guise of a mechanism geared to achieving a continuous adaptation to technical change (a productivity-achievement-reward approach), the requirements for this development are formidable. Also the point should be made that an occupationally striated system even where modified by a national redundancy payments scheme as in Britain is less adaptable to technical change than a system of structured internal labour markets involving seniority, backed up where necessary by agreements on severance pay and interplant transfer.

IV. THE ROLE OF THE COLLECTIVE BARGAINING SYSTEM

PRODUCTIVITY EFFECTS LESS IN NORTH AMERICA THAN THE U.K.

We next expand the latter point and offer some reasons why the quantitative impact of collective bargaining on productivity may be greater in Britain than North America.

Perhaps the most obvious factor, given the structure of unionism, is the higher degree of union density in Britain, at a little under 50 per cent of the labour force. Note, too, that the effective extent of collective bargaining is greater than the area covered by formal membership and union contracts (Chapter Two) *and* is proportionately greater in Britain. Also, as Ulman [41] has noted, the legal extension of the effective area of collective bargaining by Wages Councils and Fair Wage Resolutions "quite probably exerts some depressing influence on plant productivity." We should add in this connection that nationalized industries and local authorities often try to impose 'union labour only' clauses in contracts with suppliers. Local authorities have shown more interest in such clauses since the passing of the Local Government, Planning and Land Act 1980; the object being to protect councils' own low productivity direct labour organizations from the competition of private-sector building firms required by the Act.

OCCUPATIONAL STRIATION

The relevance of the dominance of craft and general worker unionism (as opposed to industrial unionism) in Britain is that it points to a greater degree of occupational striation, which in turn may be expected to exert an adverse influence on productivity. Thus occupational striation has apparently contributed to shortages of skilled labour.[18] We note in passing that the right to establish a pre-entry closed shop (i.e. that a person be a member of the union before acquiring employment) offers British unions a supply restricting device not generally available to their North American counterparts.

Occupational striation is doubtless associated with overmanning and analogous restrictive-protective practices for the simple reason that the larger the proportion of the workforce segregated into craft or otherwise horizontally structured unions, the greater is the opportunity for unnecessary duplication of work, restrictions on work assignments and analogous job regulatory practices. A classic example is the craftsman's mate (or helper). This individual is not an apprentice and typically belongs to a different union than the craftsman he is 'assisting.'

Resistance or imperfect adaptation to technical change is also related to occupational striation. Industrial unions are less likely to block technical change than are craft unions because a smaller proportion of their membership will typically be displaced by any given change. Also, industrial unions are less likely to be concerned about which occupational group shall hold the job on the new process since whoever does the work remains within the union's jurisdiction. This is not to argue that British industrial unions are free of restrictive practices, but simply to note that the much greater number of small occupational unions in Britain than in North America would lead us to expect greater resistance to technical change, delays in the introduction of new processes of production, and overmanning when the new technology is installed. *Prima facie* evidence of this is suggested by the British experience with productivity bargaining, noted above. Here the instrument was not geared to recasting the work situation into a form better able to meet technical change but, rather, to establish appropriate manning standards, shift patterns and the like for an *existing* technology.

Much has been made of the dichotomized or two-tier nature of collective bargaining in Britain as a further efficiency detracting influence. Unfortunately, the deliberations of the last major commission of enquiry into trade unionism, [15] which made much of the alleged dichotomy, were conducted in what can only be described as a crude, historicist analytical framework. Even today British analysts are divided in their assessment of the relative importance of national wage agreements vis-à-vis plant level negotiations in wage determination.[19] Given this unresolved controversy one must be cautious in attributing, say, excessive overtime working and the stubbornness of (outmoded) 'custom and practice' to national bargaining as such.[20] For example, it has proved possible to design productivity agreements at the national level for plant application. But it would appear fairly safe to conclude that an elaboration of decision units under dual or multi-tiered collective bargaining arrangements introduces greater uncertainty at the same time as enlarging the number of bargaining pairs. Accordingly, the probability of bargaining accidents and mistakes (i.e. strikes) is increased. This conclusion is underscored by the open-endedness of British wage contracts *and* the greater incidence of payment-by-results systems in Britain.

V. HOW BRITISH IS THE BRITISH DISEASE?
We have earlier identified a number of characteristics of the British industrial relations systems that make for quantitative differences in the impact of collective bargaining on productivity in Britain vis-a-vis North America. Yet it is possible that such differences between systems as were

observed are marginal. A rather more interesting line of enquiry here concerns the effect of unions on longer term growth prospects and the process of economic evolution, exploiting Britain's long-standing lag in productivity and growth.

A unifying theme of this volume is the impact of producer and special interest groups, not simply the unions, on the functioning of the economic system. We have documented the issues raised by the emergence of union political power and its interaction with economic power, the growth of a grants-aided economy, and so on. How does the historical evidence of poor productivity/lagging growth performance tie in with this body of analysis? We earlier introduced the Olson [32] thesis that the peaceful evolution of political democracy supports the growth of special interest groups and that interest group politics lead to legislation that protects group interests and inhibits resource allocation and growth — the measure of retardation being directly proportional to the length of time interest groups have had to evolve without upheaval and dislocation.

On this view, it is natural that the British disease should first strike a country that both pioneered the industrial revolution and has had the longest record of civil freedom and settled institutions. The interesting feature of Olson's analysis is, then, that the characteristics of the British disease appear not as specific to the British case but, rather, as endemic to 'settled' liberal democracies. Another attractive feature of Olson's analysis is that it does not attribute blame one sidedly to the unions but to all interest groups that have an interest in prosecuting their own sectional interests (and, as we shall subsequently argue, each others' in a corporatist experiment). Also, the analysis ties in with a large body of growth data.

Unfortunately, even a passing acquaintance with the growth literature would suggest that the explanation of economic growth is unlikely to have a basis in simple theories.[21] Olson's analysis is therefore to be seen as constituting a component part of a wider growth model that includes public choice theoretic considerations, and in which the sheltering of special interests renders economic change both more costly and also more difficult.

Finally, by way of arguing that the adverse consequences of trade unions on growth are not likely to be restricted to the U.K., let us briefly review some recent empirical evidence from the U.S. In modern research and development (R&D) studies of total factor productivity growth, output is depicted as depending on physical and *technical* capital, labour, and a disembodied growth factor. Total factor productivity is a residual, namely the difference between actual output and the contributions of labour and capital to that output. In estimating form, the growth rate of total factor productivity can be shown to be a function of the disembodied growth parameter and net investments into the stock of technical capital. In the various industry and firm R&D studies union density is appended as a control variable. Interestingly, all the studies report union effects that are consistently and significantly negative. [26] [28] [40] In other words, more highly unionized industries/firms grow at a slower rate than their less organized counterparts.

How does this evidence tally with the cross-section positive union effects on productivity noted in the section on "Productivity in the Union and Nonunion Sectors?" One might attempt a partial reconciliation by arguing that the cross-section findings pick up the 'shock' effect of unionism, albeit an effect that is not sustained through time (hence negative time-series results).

However, this reconciliation evaporates in the context of a yet more recent U.S. study that reports that industry growth is not merely negatively associated with the level of unionization but also with *changes* in the level of unionization. [24]

The implicit argument that unionism's impact on productivity is really a question about the long run is underlined by the fact of union activity in the political marketplace and, indeed, Clark's [14] finding of a disproportionate effect of unionism on the profits of competitive firms discussed in the section on "Productivity in the Union and Nonunion Sectors."

While the Olson hypothesis is clearly too simple in failing to address such market structure considerations and real-world fluctuations in the political power of special interest groups in general and unions in particular, it is toward the long run that we are ineluctably drawn in discussing union impact. And it is precisely in this area that theory encourages us to be less sanguine about union effects. This pessimism is echoed in the empirical material surveyed above.

Indeed, it is a pessimistic view of the long-term consequences of organization in economic and political markets that has impelled economists and other analysts to offer solutions to the perceived dilemmas. It is to a consideration of these that we next turn.

CHAPTER FOUR

CORPORATISM — POWER SHARING BETWEEN BUSINESS, LABOUR AND GOVERNMENT

John T. Addison

I. INTRODUCTION — THE MODERN STATE SHARES ITS DECISION MAKING

Those who advocate a corporatist solution to the British disease span a wide spectrum of political opinion and economic analysis. Thus it was a Conservative Prime Minister, Edward Heath, who in 1973 made his now famous offer to employers and unions to "share fully with the Government the benefits and obligations involved in running the national economy."[1] Similarly, economists of varying (but non-monetarist) background continue to see in incomes policy (of a corporatist nature) a solution to what they see as the basic problem of reconciling *ex ante* claims and eroding inflation expectations. And then there are those of 'sociopolitical' persuasion who envision the cure to inflation in the broader context of the more effective political integration of organized interest groups. While the latter analysts have perhaps the clearer perception of what constitutes a corporatist solution, both groups stress the underprovision of restraint in 'regular' markets. For the economist, the lack of restraint is grounded in the economic marketplace, whereas for the sociopolitical analyst it is embedded in the political (and industrial relations) system.

We note at the outset that to quote Thomson: "The term [corporatism] itself, being borrowed from the past and put to new uses, suffers from diffusion across a number of analytically separate concepts.''[2] Here, we shall refer to modern corporatism of a pluralistic or bargained form, reflecting the tendency of the modern state to share its traditional sector of decision making with private interest groups. We focus in particular on the enhanced participation of the union movement in decision making.

In the following, we first outline the arguments for and against corporatism. We next document one of the more tangible manifestations of corporatism as this emerged in Britain during the Social Contract experiment. Some empirical material with a bearing on the corporatist model is then assembled. Finally, the threads of the preceding arguments are drawn together.

II. THE CASES FOR AND AGAINST JOINT DECISION MAKING

A. THE CASE FOR
In their analysis, economists have tended to stress the 'public goods' nature of wage restraint and have seen in incomes policy the prospect of defusing the prisoner's dilemma problem centrally embedded within a system of free collective bargaining. While incomes policies, themselves, have taken a variety of forms, the dominant form which has emerged in Europe in recent years has had a marked corporatist flavour. Having said this, the corporatist policy prescription is only a vague implication of economic theory rather than a clear cut outcome. Only those economists who ally the prisoner's dilemma model with the notion that unions have a target real wage may be unequivocally referred to as corporatists (e.g. the Cambridge Economic Policy Group).†

RELATIVITIES AND FREE RIDERS
But if we restrict our attention to the public goods dimension of restraint in the economic marketplace, some interesting inferences may be drawn from the basic economic model. Tobin [32] and Trevithick, [34] [35] for example, argue that

---

†Editor's Note: The Prisoner's Dilemma is neatly summarized in Note 8 of Chapter Six.

workers are concerned about relative wages in their wage bargaining and this implies not only a downwardly rigid money wage level but also a downwardly rigid rate of change in nominal wages. In this approach, inflation emerges as a neutral way of curing unemployment by scaling down the real value of all wage outcomes. Alternatively, if inflation is regarded as a bad, incomes policy (presumably of a bargained form) provides a less painful mechanism for defusing the relativities problem.

Although this argument is couched in terms of wage relativities, the crucial point of the theory is not one of relativities: rather, it is one of contract, negotiation, and policing costs. In the normal course of events it is not possible for one group of workers to ensure, via contract, that all other groups will maintain the structure of relative wages. Even if it were, the costs of policing the contracts would be prohibitive. Because such contractual protection of wage relativities is not feasible, everyone in a decentralized bargaining system has an incentive to be a free rider. That is, to protect their relative position by aggressively seeking to advance the level of their own wages without regard for the effect on others.

Why cannot transaction costs be internalized? We would expect that lower transaction costs will characterize industrial relations systems in which highly centralized bargaining structures exist and in which top-level, economy-wide agreements are enforceable. Correspondingly, higher transaction costs will be experienced in decentralized bargaining systems in which labour market federations are unable to enforce a general wages pact. But if centralization and coordination is what is meant by corporatist industrial relations (see below), it remains to be explained how externalities can be internalized under a 'policy' of corporatism if the resolution cannot occur au naturel.

EQUITY AND WAGE RESTRAINT

One extension of the basic theory is to introduce the notion of *equity* after von Weizsäcker. [36] Here 'reasonable behaviour' or 'restraint' in wage bargaining is taken to be determined by considerations of equity. Failure to achieve equity leads the group to ask for more with unreasonable intensity. Von Weizsäcker views restraint as a behavioural public good. Restraint is called for if full employment is to be achieved even though it may not be in line with the maximization of individual preferences. He again stresses the structure of collective bargaining: public goods can be provided efficiently only by collective action and if wage bargains are decentralized the typical free-rider problem emerges. Von Weizsäcker interprets the conventional relation between the central bank and the unions as a classic prisoner's dilemma problem.[3] Unions, we are told, will only pursue wage restraint if this secures full employment. The central bank, for its part, having price stability as its principal directive, cannot be certain that a policy of monetary expansion which may be called for to bring about full employment will be honoured by the unions with wage restraint. Accordingly, it will follow a policy of relative monetary restraint. There results a noncooperative equilibrium.

Monetarism is thus perceived to be a noncooperative strategy (of the central bank). Von Weizsäcker's solution is not corporatist in form. He simply proposes a modification of the central bank-union game. Specifically, he argues that the central bank should announce a constant rate of growth of nominal GNP — rather than of the money supply — for a run of years. If such a policy is pursued, the 'game' will change in character primarily because it renders more transparent the responsibility of the labour unions for full employment (than under the old rules).

As noted earlier, the essential ingredient in Von Weizsäcker's argument is the principle of equity. The institutional context is a labour movement whose central bodies have sufficient influence on wage bargaining in the various sectors to decide fairly directly the rate of change of employment. Regarding the first consideration, von Weizsäcker notes that the principle of equity extends beyond the factory gate and "must consider the interests of the unemployed just as much as the interests of the employed" — to which one should presumably add the interests of the nonunionized. It is not clear how these interests are to be articulated, although von Weizsäcker appears to assume that a solidaristic union will somehow encompass these interests.

Also, equity is unlikely to be a simple unidimensional magnitude, and the required institutional infrastructure may ultimately challenge the basis of the private sector economy (see "Conclusions and Wider Reflections"). The quest for equity need not, therefore, be complementary to the functioning of the market system as von Weizsäcker argues.

One can detect the barest glimmerings of the sociopolitical argument in von Weizsäcker's treatment, especially where he indicts the standard monetarist solution as not merely unambitious but also "an attempt to rewrite the history of the last century." Yet his treatment remains firmly located in the economic marketplace, whereas sociopolitical analysts emphasize relations in the political marketplace. Perhaps the best statement of this position is contained in Crouch. [9]

THE SOCIOPOLITICAL CASE
In common with all sociopolitical analysts, Crouch sees the particular poise of a classical capitalist's economy as very finely balanced, partly dependent on (eroding) historical legacies and constantly facing the challenge of interests that cannot be assimilated and hence either disrupt it or call for 'extra-economic' action to defend the system of exchange.

THE GROWTH OF THE NEW INDUSTRIAL STATE
Crouch outlines how, under modern capitalism, various changes, and most notably the progressive organization of economic interests, have led to a growth in political regulation. The organization of capital is said to have intensified, partly as a consequence of the process of competition, which, by punishing the unsuccessful, reduces the number of producers (sic). But his main point is the Galbraithian [15] one; namely, that much high technology and large scale industry require conditions for stability that are incompatible with both the unpredictable nature of free competition and the multitude of producing units necessary to competition. Crouch thus argues that they necessarily engage the polity.

UNIONS NEED THEIR SHARE OF POLITICAL POWER

Hypothesizing that labour has been unable to pursue its goals very effectively through market exchange, Crouch argues that it, too, has attempted direct action in the political marketplace. He recognizes that economic forces act as a partial control, but argues that the growth of oligopoly and the public sector have sheltered labour from the vagaries of competition and secured for it a relative autonomy from demand forces.

While Crouch does argue that, at many points, the modern economy is liable to manipulation by producer group interests, his principal argument is that frequent interventions by the polity have been needed to maintain the capitalist economy.[4] Moreover, once the State has acquired an active role in the economy there are in-built tendencies for this to intensify. Thus, even if intervention by the State begins as a response to the organization of economic interests, it is likely to generate further organization: social interests will have to assume a political role if they are to influence events.

INFLATION — A PROBLEM OF UNDER-REGULATION?

Crouch views inflation as the outcome of a distributive struggle for scarce resources. In particular, "the progressive organization of economic interests and their subsequent politicization impose demands for resources greater than those which can be satisfied." The process reflects the failure of certain kinds of regulation *and* the overlapping of interests between the different modes of action. In short, inflation results from an inadequately regulated amalgam of political and economic forces. Its cure takes the form of a more successful regulation of organized interests. Here, Crouch speaks of "political creativity"; namely, institutional development leading to the more effective political integration of these interests. He focuses on the union side, arguing that the more workers' representatives are involved in controlling economic variables, the more willing they will be to pursue restraint. Specific measures such as codetermination, involvement in effective national planning instruments, and participation in control of occupational pension schemes are cited as necessary instruments to secure the exchange of a degree of *autonomy* by union leaders for an increase in real *power*.

BUT THE PROXIMATE CAUSE OF INFLATION IS STILL EXCESS MONEY SUPPLY GROWTH

Interestingly, in all of this Crouch appears to concede that the rate of growth in the money supply is the *primary* proximate determinant of inflation. His main concern is with fundamental determinants of inflation. (Monetary expansion reflects the balance of power between interests within the polity). This approach suggests that the simple monetarist solution is bound to eventual failure if it fails to change the balance of power between interests in the polity.

THE EMPIRICAL SIDE OF SOCIO-POLITICAL EXPLANATIONS

In a subsequent and largely empirical analysis (see the section on "Some Empirical Evidence on Corporatism, Strikes and Inflation"), Crouch [10] sets out in somewhat greater detail the potential of his favoured corporatist solution. The basic argument is that there will be fewer strikes and reduced inflation in those situations where autonomous unions exist in a corporatist industrial relations system which is in turn associated with a political economy capable of attracting the commitment of labour.

THE LARGER THE UNION THE GREATER ITS SOCIAL INTERESTS?

Centralized and coordinated union movements provide the basis of corporatist industrial relations. Crouch here employs the Olsonian [28] reasoning that large common interest organizations not only internalize much of the benefits of any action they take in the interests of society but also the disbenefits caused by any actions they take that reduce efficiency, raise prices or reduce growth. A centralized and coordinated union movement is potentially a source of strength. Conversely, a small-scale organization receives in full the specific gain from the distortions it produces in market processes but suffers only a minute proportion of the general cost of that distortion. For such an organization, so the argument runs, the rational course of action is said to be the maximization of the individual gain from disruption.

But whether a centralized and coordinated union movement contributes to order and stability in the face of the distortions it produces depends crucially for Crouch "on the extent to which the social system reconciles it to cooperation rather than rebellion." In the absence of social changes, a centralized and coordinated union movement poses a greater threat than a weak and decentralized movement. For Crouch, the greater the extent to which an economy retains the characteristics of a liberal political economy, the less likely labour will be to cooperate in behaviour consistent with economic stability. This follows from his argument that the conditions required for an awareness of the common interest are the reverse of those obtaining in the atomistic liberal political economy.

Industrial relations systems are said to differ in the extent to which they encourage or discourage what Crouch terms "concertation" in industrial relations. Concertation is defined as the pursuit of a common area of agreement against which a compromise between conflicting interests will be sought. The alternative scenario is one of "contestation" (and inflation) which Crouch equates with a liberal political economy attendant upon the organization of markets. Concertation is equated with centralized or coordinated labour movements which possess political strength, as indexed by the ability of political parties linked with labour to hold national office. This is where the element of political responsibility enters.

Thus when Crouch speaks of corporatism he is referring to centralized or coordinated union movements operating within a political order that can attract the commitment of labour. Corporatism thus has both an industrial relations and also a political component.

B. THE CASE AGAINST

The case against corporatism is in a very real sense the theme of this monograph. We first review this case before turning briefly to consider the residual elements in the corporatist thesis, as developed above.

The basic fallacy of corporatism is that it assumes the national interest is the sum of producer group interests, or even a subset thereof. This assumption has clear implications for the functioning of the market system, which might otherwise offer the best means of defusing the problems attendant upon the manipulation of economic (and political) power by organized interests. Moreover, the corporatist 'solution' seems unrelated if not directly at odds with the diagnosis of the inflation problem accurately pinpointed in part by certain corporatist analysts themselves.

As Brittan[5] has pointed out, a producer-oriented society is likely to make its members worse off because of their apparent mutual interest in shoring up each other's special interests and protective practices: "a tariff for one industry in exchange for quotas for another and a government subsidy for a third; an agreement to restrict recruiting in one occupation, in exchange for higher entry qualification in a second and subsidies to maintain the labour force in a third; ... price controls to please the organized consumer interest, with Ministerial price controls to investigate the resulting shortages." Even though producers are at once consumers, the producer interest will dominate because the consumer interest is diffused among thousands of products and services.

Corporatist institutions are of course reserved for 'representative' bodies. The leaderships of producer group interests clearly have a vested interest in frustrating any *true* compromise based on the exchange of privileges that would benefit society as a whole.

The operation of producer group interests in frustrating growth has been treated by Mancur Olson. [28] Since sociopolitical analysts draw selectively on this authority it is germane to review the Olsonian hypothesis. Olson argues that the unhindered growth of special interest groups in society corrodes the evolutionary mechanism of the economy. Producer units have an incentive to lobby in the political marketplace to impair this natural process whereby inefficient units of production are 'evolved out' by bankruptcy and to stifle the emergence of new competition. While Olson does suggest that societies with very "encompassing" organizations, like Sweden, will sometimes do better than those with less inclusive organizations, no explanation of the determinants of encompassingness are given (and the paradox of voting phenomenon anyway implies that encompassingness should not be equated directly with union density or the size of membership), and the main prediction of Olson's analysis remains that of increasing industrial arteriosclerosis attendant upon the unhindered growth of common interest organizations. The latter can of course be expected to flourish under corporatism. In short, it is hard to see how embracing special interest groups in quasi-state bodies would do other than further attenuate the market escape route on the lines suggested by Brittan.

All of this is not necessarily to embrace the full Olsonian thesis of economic growth but, rather, to emphasize the point that the 'sheltering' of special interest under corporatism is likely to render economic change both more costly and also more difficult.

The above reasoning is consistent with our earlier analysis of the redistribution-by-inflation game, in which the rent-seeking character of the union institution was emphasized (although we were concerned to point out at all times that unions are but one sectional interest involved in this 'game'). Let us briefly review our treatment. The starting point was that unions seek to redistribute income away from other members of society toward the union for the benefit of the membership or the leadership. Rent-seeking can be channeled through two principal avenues; either in the economic marketplace via cartelization, or in the political marketplace via the assistance of the state. Unions will devote resources to these (interactive, mutually reinforcing) activities according to their relative costs and returns. It was argued that the potential is greater in the political marketplace, especially for large unions because of their voting power. But given the interactive mutually reinforcing characteristics of economic and political power all unions have an incentive to operate in the political market for government expenditure or regulatory measures that redistribute resources from taxpayers toward the union organization or membership. In general, producer group lobbying has a greater influence on vote maximizing governments than taxpayer resistance. The final link in the inflation argument is that the increased money supply route is an attractive alternative to debt creation and higher overt taxation for vote maximizing governments. In short, inflationary finance emerges as an appealing instrument of redistribution toward themselves for powerful political groups such as trade unions.

Now although his analysis agrees with the sociopolitical variant of the corporatist inflation treatment in identifying inflation as centrally embedded within the political marketplace, it reaches this conclusion on the basis of received theory rather than in an ad hoc fashion. Moreover, it arrives at a very different set of conclusions for policy. At best the corporatist 'solution' is seen as irrelevant in that its proposed institutional forms do not imply any change in the monetary system or the vote-motive from which inflation emanates. At worst, the general solution of integrating producer group interests in policy councils threatens to exacerbate the problem of inflation by increasing the political power and influence of organized interests. The corporatist treatment provides no guide as to how unions (*inter al.*) will use this heightened power. In the absence of specific mechanisms we are perhaps entitled to presume that the general solution expands the ability of the union movement to control or influence government actions while pursuing its own private goals under the guise of performing as an agent of public policy. But we should confront our analysis with the facts. Before doing so, however, let us briefly run through the economic arguments encountered earlier.

THE ECONOMIC ARGUMENTS ONCE MORE
The economic arguments, as presented above, have little policy prescriptive content, with the exception of the real wage hypothesis. Their basic rationale is to explain inflation in pecuniary markets rather than to offer specific solutions. Solutions are offered under the catch-all of incomes policy — i.e., more regulation while the thrust of this monograph is that we should have less. The real wage hypothesis is a little more explicit in diagnosis and policy prescriptive content. Here the crude form of the argument is that workers have a real wage target in mind and that if wage increases secure less than this, workers will subsequently push for and obtain higher nominal wage increases, leading to price inflation. The implication is that unions and government can sit down

together and arrive at a package deal, including tax concessions and elements of the social wage, and meet the target by
other and less inflationary means than nominal wage hikes.
Unfortunately, the real wage hypothesis would appear in its
principal variant to have been designed to make the facts fit
it rather than the reverse. [29] For this reason space has not
been given here to notions of target real wage growth.

The basic economic model argues that it will be difficult
if not impossible to defuse the prisoner's dilemma problem
in pecuniary markets unless unions are centralized and
coordinated. Yet the constraints on union action in the
economic marketplace are neglected and the objective function of unions and the union movement remain unspecified.
We are simply not told what it is unions seek to do. These
lacunae are perhaps most obvious in von Weizsäcker's
treatment. On the one hand, an absence of full employment is precisely that which is said to lead unions to push
(achieve?) with unreasonable intensity. On the other, unions
are supposed to consider the interests of the unemployed
worker despite his ambiguous status within the union.

The unconventional element in von Weizsäcker's
treatment is of course the notion that the search and quest
for equity is complementary to be functioning of the market
economy, such that restraint in wage bargaining even
though it may not be in line with the maximization of individual 'utility' will follow if labour feels it is being treated
fairly. Now it is possible to erect sophisticated models in
which the analogous construct of a *social convention* is
widely adhered to even though it may be to the advantage of
some participants to violate that convention. [2] The stability in the system reflects the following mechanism: individuals obey the convention because so many people believe in
it and take a dim view of violators, and people are induced to
believe in the convention because there are so few violators.
However, the model may admit of another stable equilibrium in which the convention has fallen by the wayside:
there are many violators because there are so few believers,
and few believers because there are so many violators. In
short, the argument does not take us very far!

The bottom line is of course that the actions of unions,
inter al., in the economic marketplace are unlikely to be the

furnace producing the heat of the inflationary process. Our previous analysis of inflation (Chapter Two) has heavily discounted this possibility. The primary proximate determinant of inflation is, rather, an excessive rate of growth in the money supply. The question then turns on the factors that have inspired this excessive monetary growth. Here the economic arguments encountered earlier are silent.

III. THE SOCIAL CONTRACT

A CORPORATIST EXPERIMENT

The difficulties encountered by the Wilson government in the late 1960s, not least in the area of trade union reform (see below), seem to have convinced the Labour Party that a future Labour administration would require the acquiescence of the unions to operate effectively. The price of that acquiescence was conceding to the unions a say in governmental decision making. A Trades Union Congress (TUC) - Labour Party Liaison Committee was duly formed in 1972 to negotiate the shape and content of the 'social contract' to be put into operation when Labour next regained power.

Following the defeat of the Heath Conservative administration in March 1974, a minority Labour government set about the application of this compact.

In June 1974, the TUC issued its policy statement *Collective Bargaining and the Social Contract*, in which it recommended to its member unions that wage increases should be geared solely to increases in the cost of living and that the interval between settlements should be a full twelve months. In the interim, the government had promised to repeal the 1971 Industrial Relations Act (see below), also pledging itself to policies designed to help low-income groups and to maintain full employment.

In July of the following year, the TUC produced a report (*The Development of the Social Contract*) containing guidelines for the conduct of collective bargaining in the following twelve months. Indeed, these guidelines formed the basis of the government's attempt to control the rise in incomes: the TUC guidelines were simply appended to the White Paper (*The Attack on Inflation*, Cmnd. 6151).[6]

Phase II of this more formal compact was ushered in following a further TUC policy statement (*The Social Contract 1976-77*). Again the TUC pay guidelines[7] were attached to the relevant White Paper (*The Attack on Inflation – The Second Year*, Cmnd. 6507), issued in June 1976.

Phase III followed a renegotiation of the terms of the Social Contract by the TUC — Labour Party Liaison Committee. The policy document, *The Next Three Years and the Problem of Priorities*, issued in October 1976, presaged a loosening of the controls program, with the government's White Paper (*The Attack on Inflation after 31st July 1977*, Cmnd. 6882) appealing for *individual* union settlements to be consistent with a maximum increase of 10 per cent in national earnings. The twelve-month rule was retained, and government offered tax concessions.

The government unilaterally introduced what it somewhat idiosyncratically termed 'stage four' of the social contract in July 1978. The details set out in the relevant White Paper[8] did not attract the support of the TUC, however, and were subsequently modified in January of the following year following pressure from that body to allow greater flexibility.

SOCIAL CONTRACT BREAKS DOWN

The social contract experiment was not continued into 1979. Instead, an altogether looser agreement, popularly referred to as the "concordat," was issued in February 1979 following joint TUC — government talks. The agreement set a target for price inflation (sic) of 5 per cent (or better) for 1982, while the unions promised to limit strikes and picketing and to loosen closed shop arrangements.

The rest is history. After an electorally damaging series of public sector strikes, beginning in 1978 and continuing into 1979 (the so-called 'Winter of Discontent' episode), the Labour government was forced into a general election in May 1979, and was replaced by a Conservative administration pledged to policies that were remarkably uncorporatist in form.

A LEGACY OF LAW TAILOR-MADE TO UNION DEMANDS

The above account presents the bare bones of the social contract experiment, viewed from the perspective of incomes policy. While the various wage stipulations of that policy bear the imprimature of the TUC there is very little in this account to suggest that organized labour gained from the arrangement. Yet gain it did. The gains accrued in the area of labour law, namely in enactments virtually tailor-made to union requirements. The principal measures extending the powers of trade unions were the Trade Union and Labour Relations Acts of 1974 and 1976. The former conceded the unions' main demand, namely repeal of the 1971 Industrial Relations Act and its policing agency the Industrial Relations Court. In fact, in the Bill setting out the legislation it was also proposed to grant unions immunity from tort actions where, in furtherance of a trade dispute, a union had induced others to break a commercial contract. This particular clause was defeated in the Commons only to be reinstated under the Trade Unions and Labour Relations (Amendment) Act of 1976.

A MUSHROOMING OF THE CLOSED SHOP

The 1974/76 Acts also repealed all previous statutory limitations on closed and union shops, as laid down in the 1971 Industrial Relations Act. That is to say, the pre-existing qualified statutory right of an employee not to belong to a union was removed. The 1976 Act further whittled away the rights of individual union members. Under the 1974 Act such members had legal protection from exclusion or expulsion from a union in cases of arbitrary or unreasonable discrimination. Under the 1976 Act, individuals now only had recourse to a nonstatutory independent review body, all of whose members were nominated by the TUC.

As a result of this and other legislation,[9] the costs of enforcing and policing union monopoly were unambiguously reduced. Not surprisingly, there followed a large increase in the number of closed shop agreements.

In 1963, some 3.75 million British workers, or 16 per cent of employees, were covered by pre and post-entry closed shop agreements. [24] Data provided by Gennard, Dunn and Wright [17] suggest that at least 1.4 million additional employees became subject to compulsory unionism between 1963 and 1980, during which period the number of employees was declining. Accordingly, the proportion of workers covered by the closed shop rose from 16 to at least 23 per cent. The growth of the closed shop is in fact more pronounced than these figures suggest because of the shrinkage of a number of industries (e.g. coal mining) in which the closed shop was already strongly entrenched. The bulk of the growth in closed shop coverage was via post-entry shops.

There is some evidence to suggest that Gennard, Dunn and Wright's figures understate the growth of the closed shop over the period in question. This is because the authors experienced difficulty in tracing written union membership agreements which proliferated after the 1974 Act. Research by Jackson [18] points to some 5 million workers being covered by such contracts. Jackson concludes that approximately 7 million workers (rather than the 5.2 million estimate of Gennard, Dunn and Wright) were covered by the closed shop in 1978.

Using data on written agreements, one can trace a flurry of closed shop activity following the passage of the Trade Union and Labour Relations Acts of 1974 and 1976. While some of these agreements merely formalized an existing closed shop arrangement, it is not in doubt that the growth in written agreements reached a peak in 1976-1977. [16]

MANAGEMENT COMPLICITY

We have earlier noted that the 1974 and 1976 Acts were virtually tailor-made to trade union requirements. (Some parts of the legislation were based on drafts provided by the TUC staff and its academic advisers.) This is not to say that employers, particularly the larger firms, maintained a uniformly hostile stance to the closed shop. On the contrary, many employers saw the legislation as introducing greater certainty into British industrial relations. Indeed, some observers have argued that employer support for the closed shop provides *prima facie* evidence of collusion between management and unions to raise pay awards to inflationary levels. This allegation requires further investigation, but makes the useful point that management and labour are not always engaged in an adversary relationship, particularly where the consumer is concerned.

MANAGEMENT OPPOSITION TO "INDUSTRIAL DEMOCRACY"
Other facets of the social contract experiment were less readily acquiesced in by employers. Thus they actively opposed both the terms of reference and eventual findings of the Bullock Committee of Inquiry on Industrial Democracy. In 1975 the Labour government had established this Committee with the following terms of reference:

> Accepting the need for a radical extension of industrial democracy in the control of companies by means of representation on boards of directors, and accepting the essential role of trade union organisations in this process, to consider how such an extension can be best achieved, taking into account in particular the proposals of the Trades Union Congress. . . .[10]

The issues in this inquiry were thus prejudged.

The Bullock Committee proposed *inter al.* that for companies employing more than 2,000 workers there should be a number of union representatives equal to the number of shareholder representatives on the main policy board of the company. The Committee's recommendations were subsequently watered down by the government in its 1978 White Paper *Industrial Democracy*. Thus, for example, one-third employee representation on a *supervisory board* was recommended in preference to Bullock's equal representation on a *unitary* board. But, in a very real sense the differences between Bullock and the White Paper were cosmetic. Thus the one-third employee representation proposal was stated in the White Paper to be a "reasonable first step." Also, the rights of minority unions and nonunion workers were no more protected under the White Paper than they were under Bullock. Given the TUC role in framing the

White Paper this latter result is less than surprising. Trade unions exist to further the interests of their leaderships and memberships.[11] In pursuance of this goal they are logically dismissive of the interests of competing or free-rider[12] nonunionists. The only relevant consideration here is whether the TUC should have had such a dominant role in the framing of the White Paper. (We do not here address the crucial role of property rights in the efficient running of enterprises).[13]

Enough has been said to illustrate the legislative gains secured by the unions under the social contract experiment. Now there is nothing new in unions seeking to extend or protect their monopoly power in the labour market via the exertion of political power. Indeed, the promotion of trade union power by legislation can be traced back to 1900 when the TUC decided to establish a distinct Labour Group in the British Parliament. (This led to the formation of the Labour Representation Committee, which became the Labour Party in 1906). The Group's remit was "to co-operate with any other party which for the time being may be engaged in promoting legislation in the direct interest of labour, and be equally ready to be associated with any party in opposing measures having the opposite tendency." Beneficial legislation followed soon thereafter in the form of the Trade Disputes Act of 1906, which to quote Dicey, [13] made "a trade union a privileged body immune from the ordinary laws of the land." Further immunities were obtained and other legislation promoted (e.g. the Nationalization Acts) that increased the economic power base of the unions.

The social contract experiment represents a further link in the chain of the promotion of union power by legislation. At other times, unions have used their power negatively to block union reform. The most obvious recent illustration is provided by the Wilson (Labour) government's proposed Bill on union reform in 1969. In that year, the Labour government sought to set the role of trade unions within a firmer framework of law than had hitherto existed. In its White Paper, *In Place of Strife*, the government sought in particular to order a conciliation pause in the case of 'serious' unconstitutional strikes *and* to order a strike ballot of all members. The sanction took the form of financial penalties on union members where the latter failed to comply with the relevant ministerial orders.

The unions strenuously resisted the proposed measures. Against the background of union opposition, the proposals failed to find support among Party back-bench MPs (of whom over 100 are union sponsored) and in the National Executive Committee (in which the unions automatically fill approximately 40 per cent of the seats). The Prime Minister thus lacked the backing within his own party to place on the statute book reforms which he had earlier claimed to be "vital" for national economic efficiency.

The second example relates not to the blockage of union reform legislation but rather to noncompliance with existing legislation; in this case the Industrial Relations Act of 1971.[14] The basic strut of the Act was registration: the previously unconditional legal privileges and immunities of the unions were made conditional upon their registration. The crucial condition of registration was that union rules contain minimum safeguards for their members' rights. As noted earlier, nonregistration entailed a loss of sizeable legal privileges.

The TUC instructed its affiliates not to register — the price of noncompliance with this directive being explusion from the TUC. The engineering union (AUEW) for its part refused to accept the jurisdiction of the Industrial Relations Court, while in another celebrated challenge to the authority of the Court five dockworker stewards were committed to prison for contempt only to be released, after considerable strike activity, by the Law Lords ruling that trade unions were responsible for the actions of their stewards. Despite the modesty of this reformist legislation, these confrontations and the scale of union opposition successfully neutralized the Act.

What of wage developments during the social contract experiment? If we go on the evidence from past 'incomes policies,' it might seem safe to conclude that the social contract altered the time path but not the magnitude of nominal wage change. This statement is speculative in the absence of substantive econometric tests of the period as a whole. Moreover, it fails to address the issue of the pronounced deepening in the degree of union monopoly power as a result of the legislation described above. The latter should presumably be associated with a higher equilibrium wage in the union sector and, given rigidities elsewhere in the system, higher unemployment — a rising natural rate of unemployment.

We have evidence of a substantial rise in the union-nonunion wage differential for the period during the first half of the 1970s. [23] We also have evidence of a steadily rising natural rate of unemployment over the social contract period; namely, from 4.5 per cent in 1971 to 7.0 per cent in 1977. Yet the empirical link between movements in the differential and equilibrium unemployment is less than transparent. Thus Nickell [27] fails to detect any consistent influence of 'wage push' (proxied by the differential). On the other hand, Minford [25] has argued, in a rather different model, that union monopoly power (proxied by the unionization rate) increased substantially in the 1960s and the 1970s causing a substantial rise in both real wages and the natural rate of unemployment.

Clearly, more analysis of the specific effects of the social contract experiment is called for. In the interim one thing is clear: as with other controls, the effects of the social contract extended beyond its life. The heritage effects of the contract much exercised the succeeding Conservative administration, and contributed to the difficulty it faced in controlling public expenditure growth. The issue here is not really a technical one. We have noted earlier that, in the wake of the social contract, the winter of 1978-1979 was marked by an electorally damaging series of public sector strikes. The term 'electorally damaging' refers to the erosion of the public perception that only a Labour government could 'handle' the unions; a perception that had gained credence as the result of Mr. Heath's electoral defeat in 1974, largely at the hand of the miners. To settle these strikes the Labour government of Mr. Callaghan conceded wage increases in excess of 10 per cent in the public sector *coupled* with the establishment of a Comparability Commission which could award future pay increases to the striking unions in central and local government on the basis of the merits of their claim. It is now widely accepted that this two-bite offer was politically motivated. Equally, the Conservative opposition pledged itself to uphold the pay recommendations of the Comparability Commission. Subsequently, the civil servants were awarded a 25 per cent salary increase and the public sector received some 30 per cent on average.

These facts have more to do with the arbitrary imposition of pay controls and accompanying distortions than with the social contract per se. But they form an essential ingredient in any economic analysis of the social contract, albeit one subordinate to the more important issue of deepening monopoly power.

IV. SOME EMPIRICAL EVIDENCE ON CORPORATISM, STRIKES AND INFLATION

Given the imprecision and informal nature of the corporatist models, it is less than surprising that empirical tests of the corporatist thesis are sparse. We consider the limited evidence on strikes and inflation in turn.

Crouch [10] examines the links between the number of workers involved in strikes per thousand workers (annual averages, 1965-1977) and various corporatist industrial relations proxies and social democratic indicators across a sample of 17 industrialized nations. Crouch subjectively defines four corporatist industrial relations (dummy) variables; namely, centralization of the union movement, shop floor autonomy, employer coordination, and the presence of work councils. The first, third and fourth variables are taken to be concertative institutions in the language of the section on "The Cases For and Against 'Tripartite' Decision Making," while the presence of shop floor autonomy is said to frustrate national coordination and is subsequently indexed as an absence of shop-floor autonomy. All four variables are highly correlated, and for this reason Crouch investigates the impact of each on strikes separately. It is argued that in noncorporatist nations strikes are positively related to union density, on each measure.

Crouch next regresses strikes on his two social democratic variables, namely the percentage of cabinet seats held by Labour parties (L) and government revenue as a proportion of GNP less defense spending (T) — so-called social democratic 'inputs' and 'outputs.' Both variables are negatively related to the strikes variable in separate equations (although they are collinear, $r_{LT} = 0.65$).

While there are a number of statistical difficulties with Crouch's treatment, [15] some support for his basic argument is offered by the political analyst Hibbs, [21] who contends that long-run changes in the *volume* of industrial conflict (defined as man-days lost per thousand wage and salary earners — equals strike frequency x duration x size) are explained by the effectiveness of social democratic and labour parties in socializing the consumption and final distribution of national income. In this way, so the argument runs, "the distribution struggle is shifted away from the marketplace where allocation takes place through collective bargaining, to the public arena where labour can compete through political negotiation and electoral mobilization."

Hibbs reports that changes in strike volume in his 11-country sample, measured as the individual country postwar mean minus the interwar mean, are negatively correlated with coterminous changes in Socialist-Labour and Communist percentage cabinet representation ($r = -0.96$). Hibbs sees this correlation as reflecting the welfare state/ redistributive policies of social democratic regimes. The relevant simple correlation coefficients are (a) $r = 0.83$ between changes in government representation of left-wing groups and the change in public sector allocation (nondefense government expenditure as a proportion of GNP), and (b) $r = -0.79$ between changes in public sector allocation and changes in strike volume.

Hibbs suggests that trade unions have given up struggling over the market wage in those countries where a withering away of the strike is observed. He argues that public consumption is a preferable substitute for private consumption (on the rationale that labour has voted for left wing parties); that high and steeply progressive taxes have discouraged major efforts being put into fights over nominal wage increases; and that organized labour has sought to maximize its objectives by focusing on that area — the political marketplace — where the payoff is the greater.

Yet in a *dynamic* analysis of industrial conflict in ten advanced nations, covering the period 1950-1969,

Hibbs [19] fails to detect any significant impact of socialist or labour parties on strikes. While he finds strong support for an economic model of strikes, [16] supplementary political variables perform poorly. During the postwar interval, left-wing governments have apparently proved no more success-ful than their centre or right-wing counterparts in discour-aging short-run upward movements in strike activity, not-withstanding their electoral ties to the working class.

Hibbs shows that the parameters of his mixed econ-omic-political model do not vary across types of industrial relations systems (depicted as either highly centralized, centralized, or decentralized). This result is to be contrasted with other, less sophisticated treatments (e.g. Davies, 1983). So, although the mean level of strikes varies strongly with the degree of centralization in collective bargaining, the structural parameters governing the impact of economic and other variables are approximately equal across diverse sys-tems of industrial relations.

There is a problem in reconciling Hibbs' two studies. They can be partially reconciled to the extent that his earlier study focuses on short-term, year-to-year fluctuations in strike volume while his later study is concerned with long-run trends in strike volume. Moreover, the intercept terms of the dynamic study differ for each country and presumably pick up in some unspecified manner secular influences iden-tified in the later study.

A further complication arises in the context of another Hibbs' [20] study; this time a dynamic treatment of postwar unemployment in the United States and Great Britain. Hibbs finds that Democratic and Labour administrations in the two countries have driven the unemployment rate down-ward, and conversely for Republican and Conservative gov-ernments. This provides support for his argument (amplified below) that governments pursue macro-economic policies in accordance with the objective economic interests and subjective preferences of their class-defined political con-stituencies. Yet, as we have seen, Hibbs' [18] earlier work seems to suggest that such action has not reduced strike volume, although the sign on the unemployment variable in his dynamic study of strikes is strongly negative.

Turning now to inflation, the picture becomes even more clouded. To test the hypothesized relationship between inflation and industrial relations variables, Crouch [10] focuses narrowly on the acceleration in inflation in the mid-1970s. He seeks to explain peak inflation, I_p, which is defined as the simple average of price inflation in the pre-peak year, that in the peak year, and that in the subsequent two years,

$$\text{(i.e. } I_p = \frac{I_{t-1} + I_t + I_{t+1} + I_{t+2}}{4},$$

where I_t is the year of highest movement in the consumer price index over the sample period 1965-1977). Crouch first regresses I_p on 'normal inflation' which is measured as average inflation in the interval 1965-1968. The association is positive but insignificant. However, when a strikes variable is added to the equation (specifically, the average number of workers involved in strikes per thousand employees over the four years preceding I_t), the equation achieves significance at conventional levels and the coefficient on strikes is strongly positive. Also, a single industrial relations corporatism (dummy) variable — employer coordination — interacted with union density also achieves significance. By contrast, government revenue as a proportion of GNP less defense spending (the "stronger" of the two social democratic variables) performs badly, although Crouch notes that the (negative) "sign is right."

Crouch does not actually claim that strikes cause inflation. Rather, he views them as reflecting the characteristics of industrial relations systems that in turn effect the ability of an economy to respond to inflationary shocks. Nor for that matter does he argue that the institutions of industrial relations corporatism can be transplanted at will to achieve the postulated benefits of reduced conflict and more moderate inflation. He also acknowledges that the association between peaceful industrial relations, integrated union movements and corporatism has not always ruled, citing the Scandinavian countries *inter al*. as cases in point. (We are not alerted to the possible destabilizing influences of corporatism — see the following section.) One can only speculate on what one is left with in terms of a theory of corporatism.

The notion that there is a beneficial link between social democratic corporatism and inflation is a controversial one. We have seen that Crouch is unable to demonstrate a significant negative association between his two social democratic variables and (peak) inflation, and is thereby forced largely to rest his empirical argument on a highly speculative causal link between strikes and inflation. Here Crouch nowhere considers the possibility of a reverse causation between (unexpected) inflation and strikes, although this would appear to be a more fruitful approach. [30] Strikes were of course an endogenous variable in his earlier analysis and the author's admission that strikes are an intervening variable provides scant justification for this statistical procedure.

Interestingly, Hibbs, [20] while supportive of the corporatist conflict analysis, has questioned the presumed link between social democratic corporatism and inflation, arguing that the objective economic interests as well as the subjective preferences of lower income and occupational status groups are best served by a combination of low unemployment and high inflation, and conversely for higher income and occupational status groups. The argument in a nutshell is that the economic position of wage and salary earners as a group improves substantially, both absolutely and relatively, during periods of relatively low unemployment and high rates of inflation. Hibbs contends that labour-oriented, working-class-based Socialist and Labour parties typically attach far greater importance to full employment than to wage inflation, whereas business-oriented, upper-middle-class based Conservative parties generally assign higher priority to price stability than to unemployment. Here Hibbs draws on *Survey of Consumer Finances* data suggesting that, at least until 1973, the constituency of Socialist and Labour parties perceived unemployment to be a far greater evil than inflation — and conversely for the constituency of Conservative parties. [22] Unfortunately Hibbs' statistical procedures do not extend beyond simple correlation analysis. A scatter diagram linking the average rate of price inflation to the average rate of unemployment (1960-1969) is presented for twelve West European and North American countries ($r = -0.45$). A grid representing median price inflation and unemployment is superimposed on the scatter diagram. In five of the six countries experiencing an average level of unemployment below the median it is noted that there have been Socialist parties in power (or in coalition governments) for at least two-thirds of the postwar period. On the average, these countries have experienced above-median inflation rates. On the other hand, all those nations with an above-median unemployment rate (with the exception of Belgium and "to a lesser extent" Britain) have been dominated by centre or right-wing parties. Broadly speaking, the majority of these nations experienced lower inflation.

Hibbs also provides scatter diagrams illustrating the association between the percentage of years, 1945-1969, Socialist-Labour parties were in the executive and the average unemployment rate (1960-1969) (r = -0.68) and the average percentage inflation rate, 1960-1969 (r = 0.74).

The empirical weaknesses of the above test procedures stem in part from the difficulty of moving from existential to constructivist uses of the corporatist model. There are, then, obvious problems in proxying industrial relations and social democratic corporatism. These difficulties are heightened by abrupt changes in systems (e.g. the Netherlands in 1964, Belgium in 1960), although such shifts require explicit analysis and point to the *endogeneity* of systems.

A basic lacuna is the absence of an underlying economic model (with the exception of Hibbs' [19] target real wage hypothesis). Also, the different vulnerability of countries to the oil price hike in 1973 and their different priorities and reactions is a glaring omission in Crouch's study. The economic background in question has been carefully charted by Braun, [5] who pays special attention to exchange rate policies in the post-1971 regime of floating exchange rates. Her analysis, and subsequent experience, would suggest that a simple categorization of nations as alternatively 'corporatist' or 'noncorporatist' is unlikely greatly to assist an understanding of inter-country inflationary experience. Moreover, the corporatist analysis has clearly to concern itself with other than reactions to a single event (i.e. the oil price shock).

It might be countered that corporatism is more an attempt to understand the very complex interrelationships of political and economic decision-making than (at this stage) a firm line of empirical enquiry. The difficulty with this interpretation is that the corporatist treatment ignores a number of crucial interrelationships. Specifically, government and employers emerge as very shadowy agencies in the discussion. Little or no attention is paid to their interests and role in Crouch's bargained form of corporatism. As a case in point, the Crouchian definition of employer coordination is a considerable oversimplification. In small, open economies for example the presence of a highly centralized and coordinated employer confederation can often mask considerable frictions between constituents representative of the open sector and those of the closed sector. Leadership shifts occur and should be explicitly taken into account in any discussion of, say, the inflationary outcome. This observation again reflects our general contention that the influences upon government are not unchanging but, to the contrary, reflect a shifting set of coalitions and hence nexus of political demands.

Our conclusion is that the corporatist model emerges as descriptive in content rather than analytical on the causes of good industrial relations, inflation, and their interaction.

V. CONCLUSIONS AND WIDER REFLECTIONS

The corporatist analysis has alerted us to potentially important system differences in the vulnerability of economies to strikes and in their ability to control inflationary pressures. Corporatists have also drawn our attention to the important but neglected issue of the fundamental determinants of inflation. However, it has yet to be demonstrated that corporatist variables (rather than, say, country size, number of bargaining pairs, etc.) have a positive and distinct role in explaining intercountry differences in strikes. Even if they do, the assumption that what is good for industrial relations is *ipso facto* economically beneficial or benign is challenged by the very different results of Crouch and Hibbs. The exogeneity of corporatist institutions is a further unhelpful feature of the corporatist analysis.

We have presented both here and elsewhere in this volume an alternative analysis of the relationships corporatism seeks to explain, that has a basis in public choice theory. On this analysis, the corporatist solution is at best irrelevant and at worst threatens to exacerbate the problems caused by organized producer group interests. This latter consideration leads us to two final lacunae of the corporatist model concerning the stability of the broad corporatist solution and its implications for democracy.

While corporatists criticize notions of pluralistic industrialism, their own models appear to presuppose some degree of consensus on the economic organization of production, notwithstanding distributional conflict. The question of stability of this consensus arises. In keeping with the Crouchian emphasis on union behaviour, and given the interactive mutually reinforcing properties of political and economic power, we might query whether the power of the union movement will stabilize under corporatism or whether there is a threat of trade union hegemony over the entire economic and political system. Simons, [31] of course, had no doubts: he wrote of the "awful dilemma" facing democracy from tight occupational monopolies. While critical of Simons' particular emphasis on the economic marketplace (Chapter Six) and cognizant of the fluctuating level of union political power, that this danger is a real one — or that consensus is a fragile creature — is perhaps illustrated most vividly by the so-called *Meidner Plan*, the essence of which is that the ownership of the means of production should be taken over by Swedish trade unions. Basically, Meidner recommended (a) a gradual abolition of private ownership of the means of production, (b) trade union rather than State ownership, and (c) a transfer of part of the share capital to the trade union collective. Specifically, 20 per cent of the annual pre-tax profits of each enterprise were to be compulsorily transferred in the form of *shares* to a single employee fund. This fund, "an internal trade union concern," was to be administered solely by the unions. Half the yield was to be used to increase the shareholdings of the collective, the remainder being allocated to union information, training and research. The Meidner Plan was subsequently modified in detail though not substance as a result of discussions between the L.O. and the Social Democratic Party (recently returned to office), but as Myrdal [26] shows the revised proposal brought out yet more clearly than the original that the central union organizations would exercise almost total control over the capital market and economy in general alongside their new role as sole owner and employer of Swedish industry and commerce.

It is not altogether clear how corporatists would respond to this development: is bargained corporatism viewed as a transitional state or as a solution stopping well short of trade union hegemony? In the former case, it is apparent that the distinction between modern corporatism and the earlier, conservative corporatist theory of economic organization is entirely an artificial one. In the latter case, the stability of the system would appear to rest on notions of equity, social convention, and the encompassingness of the union movement. These concepts are too elusively worded to provide substance to the corporatist analysis.

Finally, there is the issue of parliamentary sovereignty. Crouch's[17] own position on this issue is clear cut: since parliamentary sovereignty has been rendered increasingly mythical by quasi-corporatist accommodation, further attenuation is taken to be of little or no consequence. In other words, the governmental capture process, although Crouch would not view it thus, has already proceeded to the stage where effective regulation is beyond the reach of parliament. This development of course raises difficulties for the corporatist argument that government enters negotiations in the guise of a rational, prescriptive third party. It also explains why other observers have pointed to a different form, "political creativity," to borrow Crouch's phrase; namely, to give future governments more authority than their predecessors. Alternatively, if quasi-corporatist experiments are to proceed, other commentators have firmly, though in our view piously, recommended that the process be depoliticized.

The economic arguments encountered in the section on "The Case For and Against Joint Decision Making," pointed to the existence of a prisoner's dilemma problem in the economic marketplace. Our own diagnosis would relocate that problem in the political marketplace. Can the negative sum nature of this political market game be defused by some generally agreed binding rule that will outlaw it? One possibility is of course 'constitutional revolution.' The corporatist solution, on the other hand, threatens to exacerbate the very problem correctly diagnosed in part by corporatists themselves, namely the governmental capture process.

CHAPTER FIVE

MARKET SYNDICALISM: "INDUSTRIAL DEMOCRACY" AS A SOLUTION

John Burton

I. INTRODUCTION

A. THE INTEREST IN INDUSTRIAL DEMOCRACY

INDUSTRIAL DEMOCRACY
Over the past couple of decades there has been an intensifying interest in the labour-managed economy as an alternative system of economic organization to those of capitalism, state socialism, and corporatism. Ideas of "profit-sharing," "co-determination," "worker participation," "industrial democracy," and etc., have become vogueish.

This growth of interest has been especially marked in Europe, both West and East. One important, underlying, factor in this is the apparent preoccupation in some quarters with the discovery of a "middle way" between the capitalism of North America and the command economy of the Soviet Union. The example of Yugoslavia, nonaligned politically and the most developed expression of a labour-managed economy to date, is also close to hand.

A PERVASIVE NOTION
No country in Western Europe has been untouched by this tide of ideas in favour of "industrial democracy" (or however entitled). Perhaps the best-known single example is the

system of worker participation in management in West Germany. In 1972, the European Commission, which forms policy in the European Community, suggested that the member states should adopt this system as regards all European companies employing more than 500 people.

In 1973 it was possible to say that 'Britain stands almost alone in Western Europe for its lack of institutions or general support for the idea [of worker participation].' [4] Even there, the atmosphere has changed. In 1978 the (then) government placed legislation before Parliament that would have imposed the legal obligation on all companies employing more than 2,000 people to accept (a minimum of one-third) worker representation on their Board. [1] Although this legislation was never introduced, "industrial democracy" remains on the agenda of debate in Britain. [2]

IN THE SOVIET BLOC
Attempts to break away from the imposed Soviet model in Eastern Europe, over the post-war period, have commonly leaned in the direction of workers' control of industry. Here the establishment of the workers' self-management system in Yugoslavia stands as the paradigm. The abortive 'Prague Spring' in Czechoslavakia in 1968 centred, on the economic front, on the formation of a system of workers' councils in enterprises. [20] More recently, the independent trade union movement in Poland put forward proposals for workers' self-management, which would give employees the right to elect the directors of their own enterprises. [3] (Clearly, however, the "Polish Experiment" is now forced to follow the Czech road).

AN IDEA WHOSE TIME HAS COME?
However, it is also significant in this latter regard, and more generally, that the Third Encyclical of Pope John Paul II, issued in September 1981, and entitled *Laborem Exercens* ("On Human Work") called for the fuller participation of workers in management. Although an encyclical is not held to be infallible, it carries with it the full weight of papal authority, to which, theologians concur, Catholics are expected to assent.

It is apparent that "industrial democracy" is an idea whose time has come. Some economists also claim that a labour-managed system has the ability to rid the Western economies of the British disease of rampant inflation, high unemployment, and sluggish economic growth. This essay is addressed to an examination of that contention.

B. WORKERS' SELF-MANAGEMENT: AN ECONOMIC PERSPECTIVE

First, however, it is necessary to clarify terminology. The vast and sprawling literature on this topic contains numerous terms, such as "workers' control," "industrial democracy," and so forth, the content of which is rather vague.

The meaning of one particular form of "industrial democracy" has, however, been much clarified by rigourous examination by economists. This system we may define as *market syndicalism*, or, interchangeably, *workers' self-management* (WSM hereinafter). The nature and economic properties of a market syndicalist firm were first explored rigourously by Ward, [35] and extended by Domar. [13] Vanek [30] was subsequently to elaborate a comprehensive and formal micro-economic and macro-economic analysis of WSM.

FIVE FEATURES OF MARKET SYNDICALISM

This economic analysis points to five defining features of a system of market syndicalism:[4]

1. Each enterprise is controlled by its workers, which includes every member of the enterprise. The management of the firm involves a combination of autonomous decision-making by elected representatives in minor matters, and decision by (majority) voting of the membership in major policy matters. Voting is conducted on the basis of 'one man, one vote.'
2. The net income (sales minus costs, including the cost of capital) is shared among the members of the firm on the basis of distribution rules established by the members themselves.
3. The members of the firm hold only *usufruct* property rights in the assets of the enterprise. They do not have property rights of the form of the company shareholder in capitalist economies: they may neither sell off the assets

of the enterprise to outsiders, nor acquire ownership rights in enterprises other than their own.

4. Each worker is free to leave, or seek to join, a firm as he wishes; and each firm is free to take on, or not, new members (as determined by the current membership).

5. The economy is co-ordinated by market transactions: firms sell outputs to consumers or to other firms at prices determined in the market.

This system of arrangements characterizes, in essentials, the Yugoslavian system of WSM.[5] The Mondragon system of worker co-operatives is basically of the same form.[6]

INDUSTRIAL DEMOCRACY IN WESTERN EUROPE

The most common form of "industrial democracy" implemented (as in West Germany) or proposed (as in the British White Paper on industrial democracy of 1978) in Western Europe do not constitute workers' self-management in the sense defined above. Under such schemes, while employees have the ability to alter or influence corporate policy, via their representatives on boards, they do not have usufruct rights in the assets of the enterprise. Shareholders retain the legal right to dispose of their equity on the stock market. Such schemes thus constitute an *attenuation* of traditional stockholder property rights, and not a WSM system of property rights in enterprises of the full-blooded form.

In this chapter, we shall be concerned with market syndicalism in the sense defined.

II. ARGUMENTS FOR MARKET SYNDICALISM

A. INTRODUCTION

SHARING POWER

Much of the argumentation in favour of WSM has been couched in terms of sociological analysis and political (particularly, power) concepts. Thus, for example, it is commonly claimed from sociological reasoning that WSM removes the feeling of alienation, diagnosed as widespread among workers in capitalist enterprises, arising from the fact that the worker lacks an ability to control his work (this being the prerogative of the enterprise owners or their appointed representatives, the managers). Again, an often-met argument for WSM is based upon a rationale for political democracy. In the political arena (of, at least, the Western countries) the principles of 'one man, one vote' and of representative governments are hallowed principles; curtailment of the franchise, and unrepresentative government, are taken to mean authoritarianism and arbitrary dictatorship. If democractic principles should apply to government then, by extension, they should also apply to industry. WSM is necessary to replace the arbitrary power of capitalist employer decisions, and to establish the counterpart of the voters' democratic rights, at work.

SOME PROBLEMS WITH "TYRANNY OF THE MAJORITY"

The purpose of this chapter is to evaluate the economic case for market syndicalism; a full consideration of the social and political aspects of the debate would require a much more extensive treatment, if not a treatise. However, it is appropriate to note briefly here some important *lacunae* in the sociological and quasi-political arguments for WSM, not least because the issues touched upon are relevant (as we shall see) to the discussion of the economic arguments.

The influence of any member of a market syndicalist enterprise on the policy-decision process is obviously negatively related to the size of the total workforce. The larger the number of members the smaller will be the individual's influence on the outcome, other things equal. In an enterprise of (say) ten people, the individual has a relatively big "say;" he represents one-tenth of the entire vote. In an enterprise of 5,000 and, even more, 100,000 people, the individual's voting power is relatively insignificant.[7]

These obvious facts concerning the calculus of voting introduce important caveats regarding the sociological and political arguments regarding market syndicalism. WSM might replace — as the individual worker sees it — the "arbitrary" decision-power of the employer with only the "arbitrary" decision-power of the majority of the workforce. The median member may be happy with this outcome; minorities in the workforce may not. Indeed, the dissatisfaction of the latter may well increase under WSM as compared with a capitalist enterprise.

Capitalist owners have an incentive to pay all according to their relative contribution to production; in this way, profits will be maximized. The majority (say, the unskilled) in a WSM enterprise has an incentive to redistribute income from minority groups of workers (say, the highly skilled) to themselves, through their commanding position in the vote process determining the income share-out rule. Thus a minority in a WSM enterprise might find itself materially worse off under WSM. As under political democracy, so under industrial democracy: the "tyranny of the majority" might prove to be a worse outcome for minorities than "one-man rule."[8]

WSM AND ALIENATION
It follows also that we cannot predict that WSM will necessarily reduce the sense of "powerlessness" or alienation so commonly alleged to reside solely in the capitalist form of business enterprise. The source of alienation is said to lie in the *individual* worker's lack of control over his work tasks and pace, etc. The individual may sense no increase in control if a majority controls these variables. The social technology of work, under WSM, is likely to reflect the interests and preferences of the dominant coalition. Numerically less powerful groups may find themselves more alienated, and not less, as the result of this tendency of a WSM regime.

The separation here introduced, between the sociological, political, and economic arguments for WSM is in one way artificial. This is so because the proponents of the sociological and political arguments commonly claim that economic benefits will flow from the "democratization" of work, and the lessening of alienation supposedly attaching thereto. The heightened sense of "identification" with the enterprise, resulting from "democratization" of work and the elimination of alienation will, it is claimed, increase the production-mindedness and efficiency of employees under WSM as compared to a traditional capitalist enterprise. However, as noted above, it is not at all clear that WSM will always reduce alienation. If that premise is not true, then the implication may not be so either.

THE CONSUMER INTEREST

Another caveat to be noted about the socio-political case for market syndicalism is the ostensible lack of concern devoted in this literature to the consumer interest. The emphasis in such discussions is always put upon the amelioration of producer (worker) conditions, at the place of work. But Man is not only a producer; he is also a consumer. Indeed, the latter role has clear priority, as the purpose of production is consumption. The play upon "approved" words, such as "democracy" and "self-liberation" (at work), in the socio-philosophical literature advocating WSM, tends to obscure this important matter. Is there not the possibility that in "democratizing" the enterprise, the consumer — who is the ultimate employer of the workforce — may become "disenfranchised?"[9] Or, alternatively, that in "liberating" the producer, the consumer will be "subjugated?" To these important matters we shall later return in this chapter.

B. ECONOMIC ARGUMENTS: MARKET SYNDICALISM AS A CURE FOR THE BRITISH DISEASE

By the "economic arguments" for market syndicalism, I here mean the arguments that have been adduced for this type of economic organization on the basis of economic theory and analysis, rather than sociological, political, or philosophical grounds.

VANEK'S POSITION

The most distinguished economic advocate of WSM, at least in the West, is Professor Vanek of Cornell University. On the basis of his theoretical analysis of such a system, Vanek comes to the conclusion that:

> . . . it can be said that under the scrutiny of economic theory the participatory economy [*i.e.*, WSM] appears in a very favourable light, both in comparison to an absolute standard of efficiency and in comparison with other economic systems. In the context of absolute evaluation it will tend to produce solutions at or near the conceivable maximum and can reach very high rates of growth and development.

> Comparatively. . . there is every reason to believe that
> the participatory economy is, all things considered, superior
> to Western capitalist economies. . . It has a definite advan-
> tage in generating full-employment, long range price stabili-
> ty, and growth.[10]

In short, market syndicalism appears in this treatment as a
panacea for the multiple ailments of the British disease: high
unemployment, high inflation, and sclerotic growth.

JAY'S CASE
Jay's (1976) economic case for WSM is more sombre than
Vanek's. Jay does not argue that market syndicalism is
preferable to the contemporary economic system in the
West; his case "for" WSM is rather that a switch-over to
this system may be the *only escape-route* from the secularly
increasing problem of stagflation that has beset the advanced Western nations.[11] As Jay, in his diagnosis of the
problems of the contemporary West, lays stress upon the
role of unionism in the germination of these problems, it is of
particular relevance to our present concerns.

THE JAY THESIS
Jay accepts the monetarist argument that the primary proximate determinant of the rate of inflation is the rate of
growth of the money supply relative to the rate of growth of
real aggregate output. However, he (unlike Friedman, but
like Hayek) would argue that union monopoly power has
pushed the equilibrium or natural rate of unemployment in
Western economies to previously unparalleled heights. As
governments seek to maintain unemployment below this
level by monetary/fiscal means, the result is inflation (and,
indeed, ever-accelerating secular inflation). Union monopoly (via its effect in raising unemployment) is thus an underlying cause of the current inflation in the West.

SOLVING THE VICIOUS TRILEMMA
Technically, there are two possible solutions to the problem:
governments may either jettison the commitment to full
employment, or dismantle union monopoly power. However, Jay argues that neither possibility, or that of ever-
accelerating inflation, is politically feasible. The Western
liberal democracies are thus caught in a vicious trilemma:

. . . [an accelerating inflation]. . . must sooner or later destroy either the freedom of the labour market (with or without the consent of the main suppliers of labour) or the high level of employment. Since either or both of these consequences is outside the tolerance of the electorate, no government will be able to satisfy the electorate; and therefore the system of political economy [of liberal democracy] is inherently unstable. . .

. . . at present [democratic] governments face. . . a choice between politically unacceptable unemployment, politically unacceptable interference in the freedom of the labour market, and an inherently unstable policy of inflation accelerating, if not *ad infinitum*, at least '*ad* Weimar.'[12]

The only escape-route — if the economic threat of escalating stagflation to the survival of liberal democracy is to be defused — lies in the wholesale adoption of market syndicalism, according to Jay. His reasoning is that only under such a system will workers be forced to face and accept as constraints the market realities that confront present (private and government sector) employers in the Western economies. Under a WSM system, workers would:

. . . become infected with the entrepreneurial realities which confront their present employers, so that they will accept a non-inflationary market-determined environment as setting the level of rewards that can be afforded.[13]

Thus the argument is that the present system of "free collective bargaining" combined with the governmental guarantee of full (or at least a tolerable level of) employment obscures the unemployment costs and consequences of trade union action to the workers. Only by directly facing them with those consequences can the economic system be made to work in a way that will allow the survival of political democracy. This, in turn, requires the adoption of a system of market syndicalism. Under such a property rights regime, workers would be able to see more clearly the consequences of awarding themselves supra-competitive incomes. Their products, and thus their jobs, would be priced out of the market.

UNIONISM 'WITHERS AWAY'

Jay concedes that present union leaders might well be resistant to his vision of worker-owned firms, because if introduced it might bring about the elimination of the demand of employees for their negotiating services with management — as the workers would now constitute (or rather, elect) "the" management. However, he argues that it would prove extremely difficult for union leaders to oppose the creation of a WSM regime, which would transfer managerial control to their own members. He is therefore led to the prophesy that trade unionism would 'wither away' under a regime of market syndicalism. The threat to political democracy posed by the concatenation of monopoly unionism and the vote motive for monetary accommodation would thereby be defused.

To examine the foregoing economic arguments for market syndicalism, we shall take up two issues. First, would market syndicalism deal with the underlying problem of producer group (specifically, trade union) power that Jay diagnoses? Second, would a market syndicalist regime eradicate the British disease? These matters are taken up in the following two sections.[14]

III. MARKET SYNDICALISM AND THE PROBLEM OF PRODUCER GROUP POWER

A. UNION POWER TRANSFORMED

Jay argues that trade unions would "wither away" under a system of WSM. Closer inspection of the issues, however, reveals that this optimistic scenario is unlikely. Market syndicalism does not offer, in itself, any means of defusing the problem of economic warfare between powerful groups of organized sectional interests located in different industries.

The basic problem is that, whatever the system of property rights, groups have an incentive to generate rents via collective action in the pecuniary market and in the political market. A switching over from a system of capitalist to market syndicalist property rights in enterprises in no way inhibits the incentive to rent-seeking collective action.

For example, under a system of WSM, worker cooperatives located in the same industry would have an incentive to collude together in order to rig the price of their product and to gain monopoly rent thereby. The agency that performed the task of co-ordinating these price-rigging endeavours might not be labelled as a trade union. But that, in effect, is what it would *be*. The only difference between unionism under capitalism or the mixed economy, as now, and unionism under market syndicalism, is that rivalry between labour cartels over the allocation of income would not only find its expression in the labour market, as under the present system, but also in the product market.

REASONS WHY THERE WOULD BE NO 'WITHERING AWAY'

Thus, the problem that we now face in the liberal democracies, of predatory competition between organized sectional interests, would not simply "wither away" under market syndicalism. Indeed, it is possible to argue that market syndicalism might actually intensify this struggle. Two major reasons may be cited.

First, as Brittan [6] has argued, a market syndicalist arrangement would reduce the costs to trade unions of some avenues of rent-seeking. An industrial trade union of worker co-operatives would be able to use its direct monopoly power in the product market to gain monopoly rent without strike activity. This does not mean that industry-wide strike activity, and most especially secondary picketing, would disappear under a market syndicalist regime, to be replaced by monopoly price-hiking in the product market. Some groups of workers might have a low degree of monopoly power in the product market, but a high degree of strike-threat power, due to their ability to disrupt the entire economy by strike action (especially if they had sufficient picket-line muscle to engage successfully in mass secondary picketing of key installations such as the docks, or the electricity generation system). These latter groups would find it to their advantage to continue to rely primarily on their strike-threat power to extract rent, under market syndicalism.

Second, one of the major processes that works continuously to undermine the potential for both enterprise and labour monopoly in a capitalist property rights system — where the returns to individual enterprise are appropriable by the entrepreneur — is likely to be greatly enfeebled under a market syndicalist system of property rights. This monopoly-undermining force in the capitalist economy flows from the invention of substitutes for high-priced/monopolized products, the invention of new technologies by which goods having the same characteristics as the monopolized commodity may be produced more cheaply, and the entry by new firms into areas of production where high profits are being earned. In short, a capitalist economy has an "inbuilt regulator" of product market monopoly. High profits act as a signal and stimulus to the emergence of competition. Ultimately, this feature of the capitalist economy rests upon the nature of the property rights system embedded within it. Under a capitalist regime the returns from successful competition with established high-profit producers are appropriable by the entrepreneurs who initiate that competition.

SOME PUZZLING FACTS ABOUT FIRMS AND SYNDICALISM

What would be the supply of new firms under a market syndicalist regime? Before examining this question analytically, it is salutory to take cognizance of two facts. First, despite the often-proclaimed productivity-enhancing nature of worker self-managed enterprises, it is a noticeable fact that very few such enterprises have emerged "spontaneously" in the capitalist economies. Yet nothing in the legal systems relating to such economies *prevents* the organization and emergence of worker self-managed enterprises. A capitalist economic system permits and rewards successful experimentation not only in the design of products but also in the design of organizations. Why then have worker co-operatives not emerged in profusion under capitalism?[15] Second, it is a noticeable fact of experience that in Yugoslavia the number of enterprises has declined continuously for many years past, as the birth rate of new firms has been much lower than the combined death and merger rate of existing enterprises.

B. HOW DO NEW FIRMS ARISE IN SYNDICALIST ECONOMIES?

ARTIFICIAL VERSUS NATURAL EMERGENCE

We turn now to the analytical question of the determinants of the supply of new competitive firms in a market syndicalist regime. We must first distinguish between the "artificial" and "natural" emergence of such enterprises. Worker co-operatives can be borne "artificially," by the provision of funds by central or local government; this indeed is a common means by which such enterprises emerge. We are here investigating only the "natural" emergence of worker self-managed enterprises — the result of "spontaneous" initiatives to establish such organizations.

An entirely new syndicalist enterprise (as against a subsidiary established by an existent syndicalist enterprise) might naturally be created by either a group of workers or by an individual entrepreneur.

THE IMPOSSIBILITY OF COLLECTIVE ENTREPRENEURSHIP

The former possibility seems most dubious, unless organized by a trade union. Vanek[16] suggests that the institution of WSM generates the mental condition of a "collective mind" in the workforce. However, as O'Mahoney persuasively argues:

> . . . even if it [WSM] succeeded in doing so after the firm had been in being for some time, and it is highly doubtful if it could, we certainly could not expect a collective mind to exist even before the firm was set up. Collective entrepreneurship could no more be expected than collective art.[17]

TRADE UNIONS AS THE SOURCE OF NEW FIRMS

Trade unions, as existent collective institutions, might of course initiate the collective action of workers to establish new syndicalist organizations. However, it is a noticeable fact that Western trade unions seem remarkably loath to undertake such businesses. Here again it is germane to note that nothing in the legal systems of Western countries prevents trade unions from the establishment of syndicalist enterprises. It is quite true that Western trade unions (as in Britain) are sometimes vociferous proponents of schemes of "worker participation" and "co-determination." However, what they are actually typically lobbying for is the legislative *imposition* of such schemes on existent capitalist (and government) enterprises, and under which schemes the new worker directors who would sit on the reconstituted management boards would be selected via the trade union apparatus. Western trade unions are, quite evidently, less keen to actively establish new syndicalist and quasi-syndicalist enterprises themselves.

The reasons for this lack of entrepreneurial endeavour, in the founding of WSM organizations by trade unions, are related to the property rights features of trade unions as currently constituted. As Martin [22] has argued, a trade union is essentially a *nonproprietary* organization. Members do not have transferrable private property rights in their union. Amongst other things, this means that union leaders, unlike business entrepreneurs, are unable to capture the returns from engaging in entrepreneurial activity. They thus have a reduced interest (*cf.*, the private entrepreneur) in the creation of new businesses, be these of the syndicalist form or otherwise. Nonproprietal organizations are thus most unlikely to be dynamic sources of new business endeavour, of any form.

ENTREPRENEURS AS THE SOURCE OF NEW BUSINESS

This leaves us with individual entrepreneurs as the potential source of new businesses under a market syndicalist regime. Two cases of how such a system might operate warrant discussion: the case in which the entrepreneur is not compensated for establishing new enterprises, and that where they are so compensated.

Under the first of these alternatives the entrepreneur would undertake all of the work of initiating a new enterprise (*e.g.*, the development of a substitute product to compete with existent high-profit producers), but the returns would be spread (once a certain critical size of employment was achieved) over all workers in the enterprise, due to its transmogrification into a syndicalist organization. Clearly the returns to successful entrepreneurship would be very considerably reduced compared to those obtaining under a capitalist system. The monopoly-busting force of new enterprises, and the flow of new substitute products, would be correspondingly lowered. As a Yugoslavian economist has stated of their experience:

> . . . we are realising more and more that entrepreneurship cannot be avoided in a modern economy and that in order to get it, you have to pay for it. [18]

WSM DISSIPATES THE RETURN TO ENTREPRENEURSHIP
If entrepreneurship, to be forthcoming, has to be paid for, from what source is the compensation to come? Under a capitalist system the successful entrepreneur is rewarded by the consumers, the individuals who select to purchase the products of his enterprise. Such a prospect is, by definition, excluded under an imposed regime of market syndicalism, in which all enterprises (above a certain size) must conform by law to the principles of WSM. There are thus effectively two possible sources of compensation for those individuals who erect new enterprises in a market syndicalist economy: the state, or the syndicalist enterprise itself.

LET THE STATE PAY THE ENTREPRENEURS
Two points need to be made regarding the possibilities of state compensation for individuals who set up new enterprises under a market syndicalist regime. First, this "way out" of the problem leads us back to the "artificial" generation of new enterprise, by public finance. It is not a "natural" solution to the problem, inherent in the potentialities of a market syndicalist system itself. Second, there is the problem that under a system of WSM the "appropriate" level of state compensation to entrepreneurs is entirely problematic. By the very specification of the property rights system that constitutes market syndicalism, no equity market can exist. If such a market were to exist, individuals would have the right to sell shares, and others — who were

not part of the current production team of the enterprise — to buy them. Such a possibility is excluded by the nature of a market syndicalist regime; the rights of managing companies cannot be transferred by sale to nonmembers of the enterprise.

But the problem is that to determine the capital value of any business organization there must be a (competitive) market in the equity of enterprises. Under the system we are considering there would be only *one* potential purchaser of the services of the establishers of new enterprises: the state. In other words, the state (in this scheme) is put in the position of the monopolist purchaser of entrepreneurial services.

We know from economic theory that a monopolist buyer is likely to make offers that are lower than that predicted to result from a competitive market; but this is not the basic problem with the system of entrepreneurial compensation envisaged. That basic problem, to repeat, is that — in the absence of alternative purchasers, bidding against each other — the "appropriate" level of state compensation for an entrepreneur is simply not knowable. Furthermore, under such a system there would be a considerable incentive for entrepreneurs to devote their time not simply to the task of getting a "good business" going, but rather to the task of getting a "good price" for their services from the only effective purchaser — the state. The bribery and corruption of the officials charged with compensating entrepreneurs would be a not unlikely event. Furthermore, in the absence of an objective market test of the value of the enterprise, it would be impossible to determine whether such officials were allocating compensation to entrepreneurs appropriately or not.

COULD THE WORKERS PAY THE ENTREPRENEURS?
Could the members of a syndicalist enterprise compensate the entrepreneur for founding an enterprise? Something along these lines has recently been attempted in Yugoslavia. Under the 1976 Law on Associated Labour, a founder of an enterprise may come to a contractual arrangement with labour organizations that provide compensation for entrepreneurship. Under such a contract (known as a COAL, or

Contractual Organisation of Associated Labour) the entrepreneur provides at least 10 per cent of the initial venture capital, and has residual claimant status over the income stream of the enterprise for some agreed period. During this period the entrepreneur retains the right to manage the enterprise and at the end of the period he may either withdraw or become an ordinary member, without residual claimant status or any managerial rights.[19]

Can such a system generate the same volume of entrepreneurial activity as under capitalism? Under a capitalist system an entrepreneur may establish a residual claimant property right in the income stream of the enterprise in perpetuity; and may also dispose of those rights to other willing buyers as and when he so decides. The COAL system is clearly a very considerable attenuation of the entrepreneurial rights that obtain under capitalist arrangements. The horizon of the potential reward stream is greatly forshortened, and the entrepreneurs freedom of manouevre is much curtailed. We should therefore expect that the volume of entrepreneurial activity forthcoming will be much less than that which obtains under capitalist arrangements, except for projects of a potentially short "life."[20]

SYNDICALISM WILL INCREASE MARKET POWER
We come to the general conclusion that the volume of new firms and of new entrepreneurial endeavour under a market syndicalist economy, unless this is artificially fostered and sustained by government finance, will be much reduced. Consequently, the problem posed by entrenched monopolies would likely be the greater under such an economic regime. Specifically, market syndicalism does not offer any obvious solution to such problems as arise from the existence of labour cartel power. Indecd, market syndicalism might well lead to a strengthening of labour cartel power.

C. WSM NO ESCAPE FROM PROBLEMS OF UNION POWER
The argument that WSM is the only escape route from the problems posed by contemporary union power is delusory. If the mechanism for dismantling monopolies that is embedded in a capitalist economy — the activity of new entre-

preneurs — is suspended or greatly attenuated, then there is only one potential source of protection for consumers against the rigging of markets by organized producer groups: the State.

G.D.H. Cole, [9] [10] the originator of the form of syndicalist thinking known as guild socialism, was clear-sighted enough to realize that the protection of consumers against organized producer interests would, in a syndicalist society, require the action of the state:

> The proper sphere of the State in relation to industry [under guild socialism] is the expression of those common needs and desires which belong to men as consumers or users of the products of industry. . . the State must rely, to check unjust demands, on its equal voice in the decision of points of difference, and on the organized opinion of the community as a whole. As a last resort the preservation of equality between the two types of organization involves the possibility of a deadlock; but it is almost impossible to imagine such a deadlock arising in an egalitarian society.[21]

Cole's thinking about syndicalism and guild socialism thus presents a remarkable combination of clear insight and wishful thinking. He was correct to diagnose that consumers in such an economic regime would only have the state to rely upon for protection against the abuse of economic power by organized producer groups. He also evidently involved himself in fantasy in the wishing away of the resultant potential "deadlocks" between the state and producer groups. Attempts by combinations of producers to rig the market in their favour are as old as human history. They are also unlikely to disappear simply because somebody finds such disagreeable matters "almost impossible to imagine" in his particular vision.

For the economy to remain reasonably competitive, and to protect consumers from combinations, the government in a market syndicalist society would need to enforce stringently laws against market conspiracy.

We thus come to something of a paradox in the case for market syndicalism as a cure for the problems of union power. On the one hand it is asserted that the present system can no longer function because of the economic consequences of union power. Market syndicalism is proposed by Jay as a solution. His argument rests on the contention that any restraint upon trade union power is politically unacceptable or impossible in contemporary liberal democracies. But if such measures are impossible in liberal democracy because of the assumed strength of the vested interests that would oppose such measures, they would, by exactly the same reasoning, be impossible to implement in a market syndicalist regime.

Market syndicalism is not a solution to the problems of producer group power. If anything, such a regime might intensify those very problems.

IV. MARKET SYNDICALISM AND THE BRITISH DISEASE

It has been claimed, by a notable economic theoretician, that market syndicalism is likely to perform in a superior fashion to the contemporary Western system. Specifically, it is claimed that market syndicalism will produce less inflation, less unemployment, and more rapid economic growth. What is the validity of these claims?

A. INFLATION UNDER MARKET SYNDICALISM
The proximate determinant of the rate of inflation, whatever the particular politico-economic regime, is the rate of growth of the money supply relative to the rate of growth of real output. The question of how the imposition of a market syndicalist regime will affect the inflationary propensities of the economy thus are a matter of how such a regime will affect the demand for, and supply of, monetary accommodation.

First, the effects upon the supply of monetary accommodation. Presumably the democratic politicians in a market syndicalist society would be propelled by the same vote motive as their counterparts today. They would have a political incentive to indulge in deficit finance and monetary expansion for purposes of political profit. A system of WSM would do nothing to alter or to inhibit such political motives and actions.

Would, however, market syndicalism curtail the demand for monetary accommodation? There is, in fact, no reason to believe that important lobbies would find the inflation tax, as a means of redistributing income to themselves, any less attractive than formerly.

YUGOSLAVIA — THE PROOF OF THE PUDDING

The experience of Yugoslavia is relevant — and in fact quite salutory — on this matter. Over the entire period 1950-1975, Yugoslavia experienced a higher mean rate of inflation than any other country in Europe, with the singular exception of Iceland — an inflation problem far worse than that experienced by any of the capitalist liberal democracies whose stability Jay argues to be so threatened by inflation. Even if we look only at the period for 1971-1975 — the period when worries about the stability of democracy under sustained inflation was beginning to emerge — Yugoslavia's inflation rate (of 19.51 per cent per annum during this period) was typically double or treble that of such major capitalist liberal democracies as France, West Germany, Italy, and the United States. [16] Even the U.K. — which Jay took as the paradigm contemporary example of the inflationary propensities of a system of liberal democracy combined with monopoly unionism — had an inflation rate for the period 1971-1975 running at a mean annual level of under two-thirds of that occurring in Yugoslavia. Yet Jay was recommending that the U.K. economy be transformed into a Yugoslav-style economic system in order to "solve" the inflation problem!

Why has Yugoslavia experienced this endemic problem of inflation? Being a one-party state the ruling political party in Yugoslavia cannot be said to have a *vote* motive for the adoption of such inflationary policies. However, even the rulers of non-electoral regimes have a survival-in-office motive — for political competition often takes forms other than that of open elections. They have therefore an incentive similar to that of liberal democratic politicians to buy the support of important groups and powerful lobbies. [8]

INDUSTRIAL DEMOCRACY AMPLIFIES YUGOSLAVIAN INFLATION

It would seem that the process determining monetary growth in Yugoslavia has in fact been basically similar to that in the post-war liberal democracies — although in intensified form, and with a few institutional differences. The forces bringing forth a supply of monetary accommodation in Yugoslavia have been basically the same as in Western countries — the workings of a survival-in-office motive, but brought to bear through the medium not of open elections but of fears of the regional break-up of Yugoslavia into quite independent republics, stimulated also by the pressures that powerful lobbying groups in the production process may bring to bear upon incumbent politicians.

Similarly, it is possible to detect the presence of a strong demand for monetary accommodation on the part of groups of Yugoslavian workers, these demands often being concentrated — as in the liberal democracies — in the "lame duck" industries. A common experience is that of the workers in a Yugoslavian enterprise awarding themselves a large pay rise, that their enterprise cannot afford, on "comparability" grounds with the wages being earned in some far more profitable concern or region. Their enterprise then gets into liquidity difficulties, and has to go to the banking system for support. Although the banks in Yugoslavia are supposedly commercial enterprises (and are state-owned instead of worker-controlled):

> . . . they, and the public authorities. . . are subject to political pressures to keep the lame ducks afloat. Though the National Bank tries to operate an anti-inflationary policy, it too finds itself obliged to expand the money supply enough to make this possible. . . In British terms, it is as if bankrupt firms could rarely be closed, not merely in problem areas like Glasgow or South Wales, but even in London or Coventry.[22]

In effect the Yugoslav economy thus might be characterized as one where there is an extremely low rate of winding-up of unprofitable enterprises, due to the political pressures to prop up such concerns.[23] The central bank is forced likewise, by political pressures, to act in effect as lender of the last resort to the "lame duck segment" of worker-controlled enterprises which are maintained by the proceeds of the inflation tax.

The important point here is that Yugoslavia, the most important contemporary example of a market syndicalist economy, has not been able to solve the problem of political pressures, emanating from organized groups of workers, upon government and the monetary authorities to indulge in monetary and fiscal expansionism. To the contrary: contemporary Yugoslavia is a classic example of that very problem.

THE POLITICAL MARKETPLACE — A MISSING ANALYTICAL LINK

This leads on to a further important point. How is it that Vanek's, [29] [30] economic theory of the market syndicalist economy generates the prediction that such a system would have a lower propensity to inflation than capitalist economies? The answer lies in the fact that Vanek considered the operation of pricing policies of capitalist and syndicalist enterprises in the pecuniary marketplace, and entirely abstracted from the existence of a political "marketplace." In the Vanek model, the workers managing a firm faced by economic difficulties would simply cut their wages. Vanek's mistake here lies in the fact that in the analysis of inflation the operation of the political marketplace simply *cannot* be abstracted from, since the proximate cause of inflation, the growth of the money stock, is controllable by government. If we introduce a political marketplace to the Vanek model of the labour-managed economy, and assume that the workers in failing concerns have the lobbying power to get their losses funded by the banking system, then the analysis no longer yields the prediction that such groups of workers will inflict wage cuts upon themselves.[24]

B. UNEMPLOYMENT UNDER MARKET SYNDICALISM

Would a system of market syndicalism reduce the equilibrium volume of unemployment in the Western economies?

DEPENDS ON OTHER ASPECTS OF THE ECONOMY

A general answer cannot be given to this question on grounds of economic theory as it depends upon other assumptions about the environment in which the market syndicalist order was introduced. For example, *if* (as earlier suggested) market syndicalism were to produce an intensification of monopoly power, and *if* we also assume that there are pervasive and well-enforced minimum wage laws, then this concatenation would (other things being equal) tend to raise the natural rate of unemployment. If, on the other hand, wages were flexible, then any increase in cartelization might leave the natural rate of unemployment unaffected.[25]

WAGE MAXIMIZATION WOULD REDUCE EMPLOYMENT

One general tendency that could tend to raise the natural rate of unemployment, if WSM were imposed, derives from the nature of the goals of the worker-managed enterprise. According to the Ward [35] model of this type of enterprise, the members of it would tend to vote for policies that maximized their wages. In this case the enterprise would not expand employment beyond the point of maximum average labour productivity.

A capitalist organization, on the other hand, is traditionally assumed to adopt output and employment policies that will maximize its profits. This implies that a capitalist firm will seek to employ up to that point where the additional cost of extra labour hired is just equal to the additional revenue so generated. This profit-maximizing level of employment, as any introductory textbook on microeconomics will attest, is always higher than that associated with the point of maximum average productivity. In other words, we may predict from standard economic theory that the substitution of an economy composed of capitalist enterprises by worker-managed firms would lead to a cutback in the demand for labour in those enterprises.

Would the workers so displaced find jobs? This would depend, in great part, on the likelihood of the emergence of new worker-managed enterprises, that took in the displaced labour. However, as developed at length in the previous section, we have seen that the generation of new enterprises is likely to be greatly enfeebled under market syndicalism, unless artificially engineered and sustained by government finance.

On the other hand, economic analysis also suggests that WSM reduces the incentives, and thus likelihood, of labour mobility. This flows from the fact that the future return on any investment made in the firm by workers (by foregoing current wages) will accrue, under market syndicalism, to the worker only if he stays with the enterprise. Under a capitalist system, by comparison, had a worker made a comparable investment in the equity of their own or other enterprises, the returns on that investment would not cease when he moved from one job to another. Furthermore, it is possible to realize the capital value of the investment by sale on the stock exchange at any point in time. Consequently, there is a reduced incentive to mobility of labour, under market syndicalism, as compared with the capitalist system. This factor would obviously tend to reduce the equilibrium volume of search unemployment, *ceteris paribus*.

In general, then, we are unable to make any unambiguous qualitative predictions about the effect of a market syndicalist regime on the equilibrium volume of unemployment.

YUGOSLAVIAN PUDDING AGAIN
Here again the actual evidence of Yugoslavia is pertinent. The experience of Yugoslavia would not appear to be conducive to the idea that market syndicalism is the solution to problems of unemployment. As Congdon notes:

> Unemployment in Yugoslavia has been very high, even according to published official statistics, for many years. The ratio of vacancies to unemployment has consistently been the lowest of any OECD country. The migration of Yugoslav workers to the freer economies of Western Europe has been one response to the sparseness of job opportunities.[26]

It would thus appear from the experience of Yugoslavia that the lack of job opportunities, arising from the lack of new enterprise, is the predominant effect.

C. GROWTH UNDER MARKET SYNDICALISM

Vanek argues that market syndicalism can generate very high rates of economic growth. The experience of Yugoslavia would seemingly bear this out. Between 1952 and 1971, the total volume of investment ranged from 29 to 38 per cent of national output, according to the year, [24] although more recently there has been a marked retardation of the Yugoslav growth rate. [28]

ENTREPRENEURSHIP OR TAXES THE SECRET OF WSM SUCCESS

However, it is not the case that these high growth rates are directly attributable to the institution of WSM. The very high volume of investment resources were sustained not by massive reinvestment at the enterprise level, but by very high taxes.

Furthermore, it is a mistake to conceive of the growth process purely in terms of the aggregative perspective of total inputs and total outputs. A somewhat more Darwinian perspective is necessary to understand the complex processes of economic evolution. [2] Progress in the economy springs from the emergence of "mutations" and new enterprises — firms with new products, different technology, new methods of organization or accounting, and so forth. Many of these new entities fail to survive. They disappear because they fail the test of economic natural selection that operates in a market economy: only those firms which achieve and maintain positive profits can survive. Firms that fail to achieve such profits disappear via compulsory liquidation or voluntary wind-up. In this way inefficient, unsound, or badly-managed enterprises are weeded out over time. The process of economic natural selection plays the vital role of erasing entrepreneurial mistakes, and of rewarding correct entrepreneurial plans. In this way overall economic performance is maintained and enhanced in a market economy.

How would market syndicalism affect the vigour of this evolutionary process? First, as noted in the foregoing section, there are reasons for believing that the institution of market syndicalism will reduce the inflow of new enterprises to the economic arena. However, there is no reason why WSM should in itself result in the erosion of the vigour of the bankruptcy mechanism. In a properly run market syndicalist economy, those co-operatives which failed to cover costs would disappear, no less than in a properly constituted capitalist economy.

However, it is the fact that in both capitalist economies and the market syndicalist environs of Yugoslavia, governments have yielded on many occasions to producer lobbies located in failing enterprises to bail them out. Moreover, as we have seen, this problem is particularly acute in Yugoslavia.

WSM RETARDS GROWTH AND CHANGE

In conclusion, then, there is no reason for believing that market syndicalism provides some dramatic solution to the problem of promoting a faster pace of economic evolution. By enfeebling the possibilities of capitalist entrepreneurship, it would more likely retard the long-term pace and prospects of economic evolution.

V. SOME GENERAL CONCLUSIONS

SYNDICALISM NO SOLUTION

The basic themes of our foregoing discussion may be summarized with brevity. First, market syndicalism offers no solution in itself to the problems attendant upon the manipulation of economic and political power by organized producer group interests, and could very well intensify those problems. It bears remarking that this conclusion is not exactly new. The dangers of the possible exploitation of consumers by producers in a syndicalist regime were pointed to long ago by Austro-Marxists such as Bauer. [5]

Second, there are no good reasons for believing that market syndicalism comprises some remarkable solution to the British disease. It cannot do anything of itself to reduce inflation, because changing the property rights system does not imply any change in the monetary system or the vote motive, from which inflation emanates. It does not offer any obvious panacea for problems of high unemployment. And by inhibiting and enfeebling the entrepreneurial process, market syndicalism could seriously damage both employment and growth prospects. Temporarily, if not for some considerable time, these deleterious effects might be covered up by infusions of public finance, to stimulate employment in worker co-operatives, and to "buy" entrepreneurial services. In other words, market syndicalism would need to become *subsidized* syndicalism, with entrepreneurs spending their time (if not some of their cash) lobbying bureaucrats for the allocation of "venture subsidies." The long-term deleterious consequences to economic evolution of such a scenario presumably do not have to be spelled out in detail. Suffice it to say that this is a prescription for, and not a solution to, the British disease.

The case for worker participation, market syndicalism and "industrial democracy" etc. is now being advocated, most especially in Europe, by a variety of authorities for a variety of reasons: "Social justice;" the "liberation of man;" as a cure-all for the British disease; etc. It is pertinent to note, however, that political panaceas sometimes do not work; and sometimes also have effects quite contrary to those intended by their advocates. An old German adage is appropriate: 'we should be careful in what we wish for; we may actually get it.'

CHAPTER SIX

CAPITALISM, DEMOCRACY AND THE PROBLEM OF ORGANIZED SECTIONAL INTERESTS

John Burton

I. VISIONS OF THE DEMISE OF CAPITALISM

It is an interesting fact that some of the most influential economic thinkers and writers of the last century or so were prophets of the downfall of capitalism. Marx foretold of the overthrow of the capitalist order by proletarian revolutions in the industrial societies. Keynes looked forward to the euthanasia of the rentier in some imminent "stationary state" of the economy. His chief American disciple, Alvin Hansen, somewhat more gloomily foresaw a disappearance of investment opportunities leading to secular stagnation in the capitalist economies, the avoidance of which would require permanently massive levels of government spending. Schumpeter diagnosed the demise of capitalism at the hands of the intellectuals.

None of these visions have yet come to pass. Revolutionary upheaval has not occurred in the advanced Western countries, even if it has occurred in less-developed countries. Nor, evidently, have we yet achieved the stationary state; the winds of innovation and entrepreneurship continue to flurry in the (so-called) capitalist economies. The American frontier may not provide the vent for investment opportunities that it did a century ago (a factor on which Hansen laid such stress in his analysis), but vast new frontiers for investment have opened up: currently in computing technology, data processing, genetic engineering, automation and robotics, and much else besides. Nor have the socialist intelligentsia yet succeeded in spreading total disaffection with the market economy. To the contrary, recent decades have seen the revivification of classical liberal ideas, and the growth of the ranks of both the libertarian and conservative intelligentsia.

Capitalism has not yet fallen, by any of these long-heralded routes. Yet, equally clearly, there is some sort of malaise in the capitalist countries in at least the West (Japan and the "market oasis" countries of south-east Asia — such as Taiwan, Singapore, Hong Kong — do not appear to be in quite the same boat). Many of these countries seem to have caught the British disease of high(er) unemployment, high(er) inflation, and slow(er) growth.

What "really" has gone wrong? This chapter explores a tentative answer to that question. I shall argue that the prophets of the demise of capitalism ignored the role of two crucial forces in the emergence of the contemporary Western malaise: the growing influence of organized sectional interest groups, such as trade unions, and the growth of government regulation, over the Twentieth Century.[1]

II. THE SIMONS' THESIS: THE DESTRUCTION OF CAPITALISM AND DEMOCRACY BY UNIONISM

In evaluating the role of organized sectional interests in the evolution of the contemporary malaise, it is useful to start by an evaluation of the ideas of Henry C. Simons on the long-term implications of unionism for the survival of the market economy and liberal democracy.

Like so many others of the great economists of the past century, Simons was not sanguine regarding the survival of economic and political freedom in the advanced West. To the contrary, his vision of the future was one of gloomy forebodings. Unlike Marx, Keynes, Hansen, and Schumpeter, however, Simons laid a central emphasis in his analysis upon the role played by trade unions in the emergence of the fundamental economic and political problems which he foresaw as arising.

A LITTLE KNOWN ANALYSIS
The kernel of Simons' thesis was originally published by the *Journal of Political Economy* in 1944, and was republished as a classic by the *Journal of Labor Research* in 1980.[2] Although comparatively little known by the current generation of students — it is not often found on contemporary reading lists in economics and (even less in) industrial relations — this essay is unquestionably a *tour de force* of tightly-argued economic analysis by one of the greatest classical liberal minds of this century.

Simons predicted the emergence of an "awful dilemma" in capitalist liberal democracies such as America, Britain, and Canada that had allowed — and indeed fostered, by the governmental granting of legal immunities — the emergence and growth of a large and powerful trade union movement. He based his prognosis of the "dilemma" on an analysis of the consequences of the (ab)use of the economic powers of a fully-matured union movement, both in the economic and political arenas.

ABUSING THE ECONOMIC POWERS OF UNIONS
The economic powers of unionism, Simons recognized, are fundamentally of two kinds: strike-threat power and monopoly power. He argued that the fully-matured exercise of both kinds of union economic power would eventually give rise to uncontainable economic problems in *any* type of democratic society — be this of the liberal democratic, social democratic, or democratic socialist variety.

THE STRIKE THREAT STRANGLES INDUSTRY
As regards the (ab)use of strike-threat power, Simons foresaw that:

> In an economy of intricate division of labor, every large organized group is in a position at any time to disrupt or stop the whole flow of social income; and the system must soon break down if groups persist in exercising that power or if they must continuously be bribed to forego its disastrous exercise.[3]

Simons argued that immensely serious economic consequences would flow from the exercise of monopoly power by matured trade unionism, namely the gradual "strangulation" of unionized industries, and the restriction of economic opportunities (especially as regards the less-skilled and otherwise disadvantaged groups) in general. This prediction he based upon an analysis of union wage and membership policy in trade unions that were being run in the (current) membership's interests:

> If I were running a union and were managing it faithfully in the interest of the majority of its members, I should consistently demand wage rates which offered to existing firms no real net earnings but only the chance of getting back part of their sunk investment at the cost of the replacement outlays necessary to provide employment for most of my constituents during their own lifetime as workers. In other words, I should plan gradually to exterminate the industry by excessive labor costs, taking care only to prevent employment from contracting more rapidly than my original constituents disappeared by death and voluntary retirement.[4]

UNIONS CAUSE THE DISRUPTION AND EXTERMINATION OF INDUSTRY

There are thus two routes in the Simons' analysis whereby unionism leads to economic breakdown. The first of these, relating to strike-threat power, might be termed as the "disruption thesis," while the second, concerning the long-term consequences of union monopoly power, might be called the "extermination thesis."

Simons argued that to try to contain these economic problems flowing from unionism — total disruption and gradual industrial extermination — governments would need to place effective limitations on the exercise of the powers of trade unions, such as the removal of their legal privileges. But, he foretold, there would be a fundamental problem blocking such a governmental action in any type of democratic society. This problem is that although a matured union movement may still constitute only a minority of the population, and even of the working population, it is nevertheless a *mass* minority, with the organization and ability to oppose a reformist democratic government, even if the latter is backed by an electoral majority; or even a majority of the population. As Simons put it, democratic governments appear to be 'nearly impotent to enforce laws against mass minorities, even if majority opinion permitted it.'[5]

Herein lies the threat, for Simons, of unionism for the institution of political democracy. If democratic governments cannot restore the legislative framework in such a way that prevents the practice of organized extortion and industrial strangulation by trade unions, then the ensuing economic breakdown will eventually lead to an irresistible demand for some other form of government, which has the coercive ability to resist and suppress the previously-unbridled abuse of power by organized sectional interests, and thus to restore economic order, albeit at very high costs to society. As Simons himself posed the problem:

> Organized economic warfare is like organized banditry and, if allowed to spread, must lead to total revolution, which will, on very hard terms, restore some order and enable us to maintain some real income instead of fighting interminably over its division among minorities.[6]

THE PROBLEM OF TURNING BACK THE CLOCK

Herein lies the dilemma that Simons foresaw in the path of the liberal (and other) democracies. The survival of political democracy requires the maintenance of a tolerable degree of economic order and standard of living. This in turn requires the avoidance of continuous economic disruption and the remorseless strangulation of industrial enterprise. Trade unions, once granted extensive legal privileges and immunities, eventually wreak this havoc. The problem lies in "turning back the clock" once unionism is entrenched. Democratic governments appear to be powerless to do so. Having let the genie out of the bottle, they cannot get it back in again. Having destroyed (by the granting of unique legal privileges) the competitive market order, and unable to restore it through the necessary legislative changes, the ineluctable consequence is that economic discipline will be eventually restored by means of absolute authority. Simons himself expressed the nature of this terrible predicament for democracy in the following manner:

> Here, possibly, is an awful dilemma: democracy cannot live
> with tight occupational monopolies; and it cannot destroy
> them, once they attain great power, without destroying itself
> in the process.[7]

In hindsight, and with the benefit of the terminology of
a branch of economic analysis developed after Simons' original writings, we may describe the fundamental analytical
thrust of his analysis in the following manner. In game
theory there is a class of strategic interaction situations
referred to collectively as examples of the "prisoner's
dilemma." These are situations in which, while all individual actors (who may be groups, acting together) act quite
rationally in their own interests, the general outcome — in
the absence of a binding agreement that effectively outlaws
certain strategies — is detrimental to all "players."[8]

Adam Smith's famous theorem of 'the invisible hand'
was that a system of "laisser-faire individualism," played
out in the context of an order of voluntary exchange, is a
positive-sum game for society. "Simons' theorem," as it
were, is that a system of "laisser-faire collectivism" — the
rational pursuit of self-interest by organized sectional
groups — is a negative sum game. Or rather, again in the
exotic jargon of game theory, it is a negative-sum "super-
game." That is, with repeated plays, over time, the detrimental nature of the game becomes more and more pronounced. And, in the Simons' thesis, eventually that super-
game will lead to a complete breakdown — the undermining
of the co-ordinative capacity of markets, and the replacement of political democracy by some form of absolute
authority.

III. THE CRITIQUE OF SIMONS' ANALYSIS: THE COLLECTIVE VOICE VIEW OF UNIONISM

Simons' prognosis of the disintegration of the market and
democratic orders in Western societies as the result of a
fully-developed system of trade unionism is bleak indeed.
The existence of free associations is one basic hallmark of
the existence of a free society. Trade unions have always

rested their right to exist on the argument that they are free associations. *To the extent* that this claim is true — the utilization of techniques such as violent picketing and mass secondary picketing by trade unions (in the West) are clearly contrary to that argument — the right of trade unions to exist simply cannot be denied by those who profess to a philosophy of freedom. However, if the interaction of a system of free associations in the form of trade unions spells the eventual death of the free society then we are in dire straits.[9]

Moreover, it cannot be denied that Simons' analysis rests on some fundamentally sound insights. His basic proposition is simply that 'we cannot all get rich by restricting production.'[10] That proposition is utterly incontrovertible.

CARTEL EFFECTS OFFSET BY BENEFITS?

However, Freeman and Medoff [13] have recently argued that the tradition of economic analysis of trade unions as carteloid devices, of which Simons' thinking perhaps represents the most powerful statement, is only half right. They do not deny that there is a monopoly or restrictionist aspect to unionism. But, they argue, this is only one "face" of unionism. The other face, that they diagnose, is what they call its 'collective voice/institutional response' aspect. By this they mean that trade unions are (effective) means of communicating median employee preferences and problems to employers. The 'institutional response' to this communication of collective voice, they assert, may well be to improve managerial and overall organizational efficiency, and thus the general functioning of the economy.

To take a balanced view of the economic impact of unionism, they conclude, we must assess the impacts of *both* the monopoly and collective voice faces of unionism. And, in empirical work on the impact of unionism on productivity in American manufacturing industry, Brown and Medoff [7] find that unionism *increases* output per worker by an order of 20 to 25 per cent. This is approximately of the same order of magnitude of the estimates of increase in average costs due to the effects of unions on the relative wages of their members.[11] In other words, the union "productivity effect" is positive, and approximately offsets the union "wage effect."

The contribution of the Harvard School to the contemporary revival of the study of trade unions by economists is to be much applauded. This is especially true of their econometric work. As Addison points out:

> The Harvard work on trade unions and productivity has firmly shifted the focus of investigation away from piecemeal and largely anecdotal evidence on the job regulatory practices of trade unions toward a systematic analysis of trade union impact. [12]

If the thrust of the Harvard School's contentions are correct, then we may be less worried by the monopoly face of unionism than Simons' forebodings would suggest. There is the offsetting collective voice or productivity-enhancing effect of unionism to consider as well. Freeman and Medoff themselves argue that:

> The positive collective voice/institutional response effects are, in many settings, more important than the negative monopoly effects. . . . [13]

Indeed, they appear to regard with regret the evident post-war gradual demise of American private sector unionism, in terms of union density in that sector.

IV. A CRITIQUE OF THE TWO ANALYSES

It will here be argued that both the Simons' view of unionism, emphasizing its monopoly face, and the Harvard School view, which is that there is a counterbalancing productivity-enhancing impact to the monopoly face, tend to ignore some important and germane matters in an evaluation of the overall impact of unionism.

THREE PROBLEMS WITH SIMONS AND THE HARVARD SCHOOL

First, the underlying model of the trade union employed by Simons and the Harvard School are subject to similar theoretical deficiencies. Second, both analyses tend to ignore the importance and significance of market reactions to unionism. Third, both analyses tend to underestimate the role and significance of trade union activity in the political market. We review these three deficiencies in turn.

A. THE UNDERLYING THEORETICAL MODEL OF THE TRADE UNION

Neither Simons, nor the Harvard School (as yet), provide a specification of their underlying theoretical model of the union. In Simons' case this was legitimate in that we do have in economics a well-developed model of monopoly, which can be quite easily transferred from its usual goods market setting to that of the labour market.[14] Such a rationale for the evasion of model specification is not true of the Harvard School's work. They argue that there are two faces of unionism, but the theoretical integration of these two faces, and an economic analysis underlying their diagnosed 'collective voice/institutional response,' is nowhere provided. Thus their work is at the moment rather open to the charge that it is "measurement without theory." Moreover, the interpretation to be put on their econometric results are open to considerable question.[15]

DO UNIONS REPRESENT THEIR MEMBERS?

An underlying assumption of both Simons and Freeman and Medoff [13] is that trade unions are institutions that reflect the preferences of their members. Simons recognized that there could be a conflict of interest between union members and leaders, but he argued that 'this conflict will usually be reconciled in favour of the interests of the rank and file. . .'[16] Freeman and Medoff [13] also argue that 'under the voice view, unions are expected to be democratic political organizations, responsive to the will of their members.' They also find, in their empirical research, that the 'vast majority of the evidence appears to support the voice view.'

While a model of the trade union as a member-dominated organization may have applicability to small trade unions (e.g. in the emergent phase of unionism), its relevance to the typical large-size membership union of today is open to much theoretical question.

The reality of union decision-making is that issues are not typically decided upon by a referendum of all members.

The cost of a continuous referendum on all policy issues would of course be astronomical. Thus the modern trade union, as with the modern democracy, is necessarily a representative institution. But elected representatives are of necessity given discretion in decision-making. This discretion — no less in the modern trade union than in contemporary liberal democracy — allows elected representatives some leeway to pursue their own *private* interests, which are not necessarily those of their members. The potential leeway for the exercise of executive discretion in trade unions will depend upon the *constraints* put upon union leaders by membership reaction.

A CURIOUS LACUNA
The Harvard School draws much upon Hirschman's [16] exit/voice taxonomy in the discussion of unionism. They have, at least in their more popular writing, extolled the virtues of unionism as an effective instrument of "voice," and tended to denigrate the comparative information value of the signalling generated by "exit" from an organization or relationship. However, they fail to apply the Hirschman analysis to the problem of membership policing of the leadership *within* unions. This is a curious *lacuna*, because Hirschman [16] himself was primarily concerned to erect his analysis of the exit and voice options in order to analyze those situations where an organization malfunctions, in the sense that it fails to follow those policies desired by its members.

PROBLEMS WITH DEMOCRACY WITHIN UNIONS
Where such organizational malfunction occurs, as Hirschman argued, two broad classes of member responses are possible: withdrawal from the relationship (the exit option); and greater participation in the internal affairs with a view to making dissent more well known (the voice option). Freeman and Medoff, [13] despite their extensive reference to the exit/voice taxonomy, fail to ask how these mechanisms would work *within* trade unions to ensure imposition of membership preferences on union leaders. [17]

We should theoretically expect a perfect imposition of member preferences (or rather, those of the median union member) on the leadership *only* under the condition in which the exercise of either (or both) of the union exit or voice options were costless to union members. This is clearly not a realistic hypothesis. Competition between trade unions for members is by no means perfect; indeed there are often jurisdictional agreements among them that impede the possibility of a disgruntled member switching to another union. The existence of the closed shop — which covers, for example, two-thirds of all British blue-collar workers in manufacturing — also raises the disgruntled member's cost of using the exit mechanism. Exit from the union will in this case mean entry to another line of employment or even into unemployment. More formally, recourse to the exit option in this latter situation will mean the foregoing of the returns stream on such human capital investments made by the exiting member that are specific to his current type of employment.

THE COSTS OF MONITORING UNION LEADERSHIP
Moreover, use of the voice mechanism to police union leadership is not without its costs. As Martin [20] argues, the fundamental characteristic of the trade union, viewed from the property rights perspective, is that it is a *nonproprietal* form of organization; members cannot sell their voting rights (as may stockholders). This means conversely that no member can aggregate these voting rights, and challenge the incumbent leadership in the manner of the classic business takeover battle. The exercise of voice within the trade union thus means the member involving himself in (boring!) branch meetings, which is costly in terms of time.

Moreover, while the costs of such voice activity are definite, the expected returns may be minute in a large trade union, because each individual has but the smallest influence on the overall outcome. His is one voice amongst many, and may thus be "drowned out" by the general noise. It is not surprising, in the light of this analysis, that attendance at union branch meetings is so low.

Voice can be exercised within the union by giving support to a new contender for the leadership. However, the incumbent leadership does have certain inbuilt advantages against such challenges. The incumbent is usually better known to the membership than the aspirant. The leadership usually controls the machinery of the trade union, including its channels of communication with the membership. Aspirants for union leadership, like new political parties, face a very uphill task in seeking to dislodge the incumbent "establishment." Not surprisingly, union leadership positions are seldom contested.

UNIONS MAY NOT BE REPRESENTATIVE
For these reasons, it seems unlikely that trade unions are perfectly reflective of their members' interests and preferences. The possibility exists of a considerable degree of executive discretion vested in the leadership. How this discretion will be utilized will of course depend on the nature of union leader goals. Some may wish to "wreck the capitalist system;" others to feather their own nest.

The general point is that both of the two views of unionism reviewed in the foregoing section ignore an important facet of the nature of unionism, and its consequences for the workings of the economy and polity.

B. THE IMPORTANCE AND SIGNIFICANCE OF MARKET RESPONSES TO UNIONISM

THE MARKET CURBS MONOPOLY POWER
Simons, in his chilling analysis of the strangulation of industry by monopolistic unionism underestimated, I would argue, the power of the market process to defuse the problem of monopoly, including labour market monopoly.

It is not sufficiently well understood that a market economy has, embedded within it, a process whereby all monopolies and cartels are subjected to forces of erosion and potential extinction in the long run. This is quite true even if there is no (effective) anti-monopoly legislation (as is the case regarding trade unions in all Western countries today). The very attempt by any group of producers to rig the market in their favour creates incentives for other entrepreneurs to find ways of selling at lower prices (or at higher quality for the same price) to consumers. The latter have the incentive to reward such market "monopoly-busters" by their purchases. This is the process by which markets destroy monopoly, and consumers escape "capture" by producer groups. Unless the cartel operators can obtain means from the state (or organized crime) to prevent this escape process from operating or unless they own a completely unique resource, the cartel sows the seed of its own destruction. Of course, the destruction of producer group collusion by the market escape process takes much time and effort, and thus will not occur instantaneously. But, in the long term, it can be a very powerful force in defusing the problem of monopoly.

FOUR ESCAPE ROUTES FROM LABOUR MONOPOLY

The contemporary demise of private sector unionism in America is illustrative of the general process.[18] According to the statistics of the Bureau of Labor Statistics, private sector union members accounted for 24 per cent of the total workforce in 1956. By 1978, this figure had fallen to 16.4 per cent. Meanwhile, the absolute number of private sector union members had remained virtually static. What has caused this phenomenon? Essentially, I would suggest, it is to be read as the consequence of the workings of the market escape process. The American consumer is beginning successfully to evade American labour market monopolies, with profound consequences for the membership of the latter.

FOREIGN COMPETITION

Four routes by which this escape has been effected are especially noteworthy. First, the American consumer has turned away from high-cost products coming from domestic unionized industries, towards lower cost foreign imports. Foreign competition has now taken a large part of the share of American markets once almost totally supplied by domestic industry, and which have become highly unionized (e.g., textiles, electrical equipment).

THE SUNBELT

Second, American business has moved away from locations where unionization is high to those where it is lower. Sometimes they have moved their operations overseas. Within the U.S.A., business has moved away from the North-East and

Mid-West "Frostbelt" states, where unionization is relatively high, towards the Sunbelt states (such as Texas and Oklahoma) where union density is much lower (typically less that 20 per cent). Manufacturing employment has, in consequence, been growing rapidly over recent decades in the "Sunbelt," and declining in the "Frostbelt."

EMPLOYEE SUBSTITUTION

Third, American business has sometimes stayed put, but substituted types of employee with a lower propensity to unionize. For example, there have been massive increases in female employment over the post-war period; and females have apparently a much lower propensity to unionize than males (indeed, the proportion of the American female labour force that is unionized has been declining over recent decades).

DECERTIFICATION

Fourth, many entrepreneurs have invested in measures that reduce the prevalence of unionism in their business. More personnel and legal specialists may be hired. Again, they may invest greater resources in countering unions in decertification and certification elections, held under the auspices of the National Labor Relations Board. Over the past two decades, American unions have in consequence been winning a smaller and smaller fraction of certification elections (less than half, currently). The number of decertification elections has risen dramatically; and in 1977 the unions lost three-quarters of those elections.[19].

All of this is the predictable long-term response of the market process to the creation of labour market cartels. Thus, unless unions can obtain legislative measures to impede or prevent the market escape process, I am more sanguine than was Simons regarding the long-run consequences of unionism for the survival of capitalism. To this matter we shall shortly return.

DO UNIONS REALLY CONTRIBUTE TO THE FIRM'S WELFARE?

Freeman and Medoff [13] also underestimate the significance of market responses to unionism. If, as they allege, the collective voice, positive effects of unionism on productivity are more important than the negative monopoly effects, why should management so often oppose the unionization of their workforce?

Their own answer to this question is as follows. First, they do not deny that in at least some industrial settings unionism is not 'functional' (i.e., the social costs of unionism are higher than the social benefits). Secondly, although unionism — in most settings, as they see it — generates net positive gains by increasing managerial efficiency and responsiveness to employee preferences, the managers themselves may not like the situation. They will need to work harder, and will suffer a loss of managerial autonomy and operating flexibility. Thus they will resent and oppose unionization.

We may accept the first of Freeman and Medoff's arguments — as it is a *caveat* to the general thrust of their analysis — and concentrate on the second. Other economists e.g., Troy, Koeller and Sheflin [32], have found it suspicious. Pencavel states the problem succinctly:

> . . . if management were cognisant of the [supposed] productivity-augmenting effect of unionism, then we should see more cases of firms actively encouraging the unionisation of their workers. Indeed, if this were the dominant influence, unionised firms would out-compete nonunionised firms.[20]

In a subsequent retaliation to this argument, Freeman and Medoff claim that this argument is:

> . . . just plain wrong. As any businessman or woman will tell you, the firm is concerned with profits, not productivity for productivity's sake. Unionized establishments may be more productive than nonunionized establishments, but if union wages are higher, profit rates in unionized firms may be lower.[21]

Who is right and wrong in this controversy? The answer is that Freeman and Medoff have been misled by an important insight into making two basic errors of analysis. Their insight is that managers — like any employee — have an incentive to shirk, and to avoid implementing new methods (including new methods of communicating with subordinates) that may add to productivity and/or profits, but which involve for them a loss of power or status, an increase in work-load, or other disagreeable matters.

MISTAKES AND CENTRAL INCONSISTENCIES IN THE HARVARD VIEW

However, the first mistake of Freeman and Medoff is to ignore the role of owners (as against managers) and of entrepreneurs. Owners of corporations have an incentive to monitor and police the behaviour of the managers they have appointed to reduce such shirking and to improve enterprise performance. [3] Where they fail to do this, others are given an incentive to make a take-over bid, sack the shirking managers, and introduce new managers and more efficient methods of operation. Alternatively, other entrepreneurs are given an incentive to set up rival enterprises, and to outcompete the corporation that is employing slothful managers and inefficient methods. Thus "managerial opposition" is not in itself sufficient to explain business resistance to unionism over the long term.

The real question is how unionism affects profitability — as Freeman and Medoff state in their riposte. If unionism adds to profitability, then owners and entrepreneurs would mount their own resistance to managerial opposition to unionism; managerial resistance, by one route or another, would be dismantled, and unionism would spread throughout the private sector. If, on the other hand, unionism reduces profitability, then owners and entrepreneurs would reinforce the resistance of managers to unionism.

The fundamental explanation of Freeman and Medoff of business opposition to unionism is thus their finding that '. . . the rate of return on capital [is often] lower under collective bargaining.' Their second basic error is their failure to understand that this latter claim is inconsistent with their other major empirical claim: that trade unions often increase productivity more than they cause an increase in (relative) wages; or that these two factors are roughly offsetting. If unionism shifts the marginal productivity of labour curve more than it raises wages then, without qualification, unionism must *add* to total profits, and thus to the rate of return on capital.

There is thus a central inconsistency in the Freeman-Medoff argument: their empirical findings are inconsistent with their analysis and interpretation. If unions do the things they say they do to productivity and wages — and thus add to profitability (in most cases) — then we should expect to find the market process leading to the (perhaps gradual) embrace of unionism.

The reality in America, which so concerns Freeman and Medoff, is that consumers and entrepreneurs are making increasingly vigorous and varied attempts to escape the embrace of unionism. The purpose of production is consumption (and not the other way around) and, in a market economy, consumers — who constitute the ultimate employers of labour and other factors — have the possibility of using the exit option to express their choices. And in America they have been using this option, with evident consequences for union membership. Freeman and Medoff, in their analysis of the impact of unionism, fail to understand the significance of this long-term market test of the institution of American private sector unionism.

C. THE ROLE AND SIGNIFICANCE OF UNION
   ACTIVITY IN THE POLITICAL MARKET

Both Simons and Freeman and Medoff address insufficient attention in their analyses to the role of the political market as regards the overall impact of unionism.

UNIONS IN THE POLITICAL MARKET — DAMMING UP THE ESCAPE ROUTES

The political market is in fact central to the growth prospects — or lack of them — of trade union organizations. In the private sector, set against a background of the general and erosive influence of market processes on producer group cartels, trade unions are unlikely, if they cannot find ways of enhancing profitability, of achieving great organizational growth, or even of avoiding long-term stagnation — unless they are supported by legislative measures that buttress their position. Historically, for example, surges in union growth have been linked to pro-union changes in the legislative environment. [22] Thus arises the incentive for private sector unionism to devote resources to the implementation of legal and regulatory measures that dam up the market "escape process." For the implementation of such measures they must, of necessity, turn to the political market, and seek to influence it.

Public sector unions are, inevitably, direct operators in the political market. Bargaining by unions over the terms and conditions of employment of their members *means* bargaining over the content of government policy towards these matters. [31] The public sector union may itself be seen as a form of political organization aimed at the manipulation of politicians, via the delivery (or non-delivery) of political support. [19]

The production of influence over the political market is thus of central importance to both private and public sector trade unions.

Simons did realize that trade unions could operate as powerful 'pressure groups in [on] government.'[22] His entire analysis is built on the premise that trade union monopoly powers rest upon legal immunities granted by government — immunities that, once given away, may be difficult or impossible for a (democratic) government to later rescind.

However, the analysis of the market "escape process" sketched above suggests that we may perhaps be more sanguine about the economic consequences of unionism in the long term than Simons indicated. The important *caveat to this latter statement is that, if trade unions are successful in the political arena*, in obtaining measures in the future that impede or suspend the market escape process, then the outlook is much more bleak. These measures could cover a vast variety of forms: minimum wage laws, prohibitions against plant closures or redundancies, tariffs, quotas, regulations, nationalization, subsidies, new or strengthened legal immunities for trade unions, schemes of (union-administered) "industrial democracy," union control over pension funds, and so on. In all Western countries, trade unions are powerful political lobbyists for some or all of the foregoing measures; as is quite predictable.

SIMONS' ANALYSIS REVERSES THE MARKET CAUSALITY

Thus, to summarize: Simons argued that the threat to the democratic order posed by unionism runs through the collapse of the competitive market order. Unionism leads to economic breakdown, which will then lead to the suspension of democratic politics. The analysis developed in this essay points, firstly, to a different sequencing to the nature of the threat posed by unionism to capitalism and democracy; and secondly, it suggests that the workings of the democratic political market are the central channel by which the threat emerges.[23] Monopoly unionism embedded in a market order, set against the background of a non-interventionist state, would not destroy the market mechanism. In the long term it would be the other way around: the market process would undermine monopoly unionism. However, in the contemporary West we do not live in a non-interventionist political order. All Western governments have vast batteries of regulatory measures at their disposal. And they can undoubtedly be influenced by politically-powerful organized sectional interests to wield such measures in the favour of the latter.

Thus, the potential threat to the survival of capitalism and democracy posed by unionism comes from a different direction to that anticipated by Simons. The real threat is that organized sectional interests, of which trade unions would be a singularly important example, are able to wrest such complex tangles of special-interest legislation from the democratic political process that the workings of the market economy are hampered and eventually undermined. The possibility is that unconstrained democratic processes, manipulated by powerful economic lobbies, will destroy economic freedom.

POLITICAL PROCESS IGNORED BY THE HARVARD SCHOOL

Freeman and Medoff likewise address insufficient attention to the political impact of unionism, and the indirect effects of this upon the functioning of the economy. In their major attempt to review and assess all evidence to date on the impact of unionism on the economic process [15] they ignore entirely the possibility that unionism may influence economic variables indirectly via the route of the political market. This is not to say they have ignored the matter entirely in other writing. In their 'Two Faces' paper of 1979, they briefly consider the question. Their conclusion is that:

> Despite the bad press given some union efforts to obtain special-interest legislation, much union muscle has been devoted to progressive social policy which provides no obvious material gains to unionized workers, save as members of the overall working population. . .
> . . . All in all, while unions, like other groups in a pluralist society, have fought for self-interest legislation, they have scored their greatest political victories on more general social legislation. In terms of actual outcomes, unions have been more effective as a voice of the whole working population and the disadvantaged than as a monopoly institution seeking to increase its monopoly power.[24]

It is quite true that American unionism has not always achieved its special-interest legislative goals. The American union movement has consistently and virulently opposed the Taft-Hartley Act of 1947 — which banned the closed shop and opened the door to ''Right-to-Work'' legislation at the state level — without success. Yet the Freeman-Medoff conclusion is, I would suggest, both naive and myopic, and dangerous on both of these accounts. It is naive because organized interests that seek to play the game of redistribution in their sectional interest seldom don any other cloak than that of Robin Hood, be the game played in the political or pecuniary market — or in Sherwood Forest. Commonsense caution thus dictates that we should be extremely wary of any organized producer group that claims to be acting as some surrogate Salvation Army. This is how trade unions have always portrayed themselves. The argument that trade unions require unique legal privileges because this aids the poor and disadvantaged is an old refrain, even if the content of it is more than questionable.

The Freeman-Medoff view on this matter is also myopic in an international sense. Rather like the ancient —

and recent — Chinese, many American economists make the assumption that the "relevant" world stops at their own borders. Freeman and Medoff talk only of the political muscle of American unionism, and ignore the evidence in other Western countries, such as Britain.[25]

Even as regards the United States, it would seem somewhat difficult to entertain the argument seriously that American unionism has been virtually impotent as regards the passage of special interest legislation. Consider, as but one example, the widespread enactment of public sector collective bargaining legislation by American state governments over recent decades. In 1958 no states had such legislation; but by 1979 some 37 of them had passed such legislation. Since the mid-1960s economists have detected rent elements in the earnings streams of American public sector employees. [4] [24] Could it not be that those two matters are connected? Evidence regarding other types of economic legislation would also suggest that American trade unions are not ineffective operators in the political arena e.g., Bloch [6] and Kau and Rubin. [17] [18]

Moreover, there are grounds for suggesting that American trade unionism may well intensify its quest for special-interest legislation in the political market, although the "British model" — formation of their own political party — is not on the cards for a number of reasons. [11] [32]

V. CONCLUSION

What does unionism imply for the future of capitalism and democracy? The answer of Henry Simons to that question was sombre. Unionism would strangulate and render chaotic the market economy, and stood likely to bring down democracy in the wake. The contemporary Harvard School view, at least as voiced by Freeman and Medoff, is far more sanguine. Here unionism is seen as having a collective voice aspect that enhances productivity, so offsetting the monopoly aspect diagnosed by Simons. In this view, unionism is quite compatible with both the survival of capitalism and democracy. Indeed, there is a suggestion that it positively contributes, in the large, to the functioning of both institutions.

In this chapter I have critically examined both of these views. In fact both seem to entail remarkably similar flaws. Not only do both views rest on an over-simplistic analysis of the nature and internal working of the trade union as an institution, but also they fundamentally misjudge the role and significance of both the market and political processes with which unionism interacts.

My general conclusion is that Simons was right to warn of a potential threat to the survival of capitalism and democracy arising from a matured labour union movement, but that he misdiagnosed the nature of, and sequence of events involved in, such a scenario. In the alternative formulation of the situation here presented, the cause for concern is that unions, and other organized sectional interests, through their ability to exact special interest legislation from government, will cause a sappening of the market process and general economic sluggishness, which exhibits itself (at least at first) as a retardation of measured economic growth rates, compared to that witnessed in earlier times. [23] I would argue that this process has occurred, and continues to occur, in all Western countries with democratic political regimes, with Britain serving as perhaps the most matured example of the phenomenon.

It is perhaps the implicit recognition of this problem that has led to such interest in Britain, and Europe more generally, in corporatism and market syndicalism. These two economic systems are increasingly proposed as solutions to the problem of union, and more generally producer group, power.

But to recognize a problem is not the same thing as to solve it. Corporatism attempts to solve the problem by openly recognizing the politico-economic power of organized sectional interests, within the institutions of special quasi-state institutions. This is not a solution to the problem. *The* problem is that, under the aegis of our present interventionist regimes, producer groups (especially) use their influence in the political market to stifle the authentic voice of consumer protest — the "market escape" procedure. In a corporatist scenario, producer group political influence is institutionally entrenched in quasi-state forms. Who speaks for the consumer in these councils? The philosophy of corporatism neglects this little matter. How do consumers escape the predation of organized producer groups, once the latter are brought into cosy alliance under the corporatist umbrella?

The advocates of market syndicalism also fail to address the problem. Certainly we live in a world in which there is an extensive clash, even across countries, between well-organized sectional interests, trade unions being one of the main actors in this grim play. But the market-capitalist-economy has an inbuilt mechanism for attacking this problem. The wholesale institution of market syndicalism by state action can only weaken that mechanism, and it poses *no* solution to the real problem, that of the magnified power of organized sectional interests in the political market. Moreover, by weakening the vigour of entrepreneurial activity, market syndicalism would be likely to increase the economic power of organized groups, and thus to intensify the very problem which this system is supposed (by some) to cure.

Three *caveats* concerning the implications of my analysis are especially worthy of mention. First, trade unions are not the only organized sectional interest involved in such operations in the political market. They are, however, to be considered a singularly important case of the general phenomenon, not least because of the large numbers (of voters/members) involved. They thus represent an important constituency in particular for government to placate with sectionally-desired measures.

Second, while market processes may be undermined by government regulation and intervention, they also exhibit regenerative capacities. Organized sectional interests may obtain measures from government to fortify their position against the erosive forces of market competition, but other actors in the market have an incentive to find ways around the impact of these measures also. The market escape process undermines the effectiveness not only of monopolies but, over time, of government measures designed to protect monopolies. For example, even though a government may introduce a minimum wage law to protect trade unionists from the competition of nonunion labour, entrepreneurs and employees in the nonunion sector have the incentive to minimize its impact by adjusting (downwards) the non-monetary benefits afforded by the workplace environment. [21]

Two vast social processes are thus in constant clash with each other throughout time: the constant attempt of producer groups to make consumers captive through regulations issued and enforced by the state, and the market escape process. It seems likely that the "governmental capture process," as it might be called, can often be effectively used to stem and overwhelm market forces in the short term; but we cannot predict with confidence that it can outpace the subtle workings of the market escape process in the long term. It is also likely that, to successfully quell the erosive force of the market escape process in the long term, groups seeking to sustain their monopoly power via state action would need an *increasing*, and increasingly diverse, volume of such action. Herein lies the evident danger of the whole process; but, to repeat, it cannot be stated with certainty that the capture process can outpace or overwhelm the escape process in the long term.

Third, if the operation of the capture process were to reach much higher levels than we currently experience, we cannot be sure that the organization of the political market would remain as it is presently constituted (and which allows the whole process to proceed). One possibility is that, at some point in time, the negative sum nature of this political market "game" becomes so glaringly obvious to all players that they, by general consensus, introduce some binding rule that outlaws it. In Buchanan's phraseology, the outcome may be that of "constitutional revolution." [8] However, the escaping by such means of this prisoner's dilemma, embedded in contemporary democratic political regimes, will not be easy. It is of the very essence of a prisoners' dilemma that the participants are unable to devise and enforce a binding rule; and this keeps them locked into it. Moreover, this particular prisoners' dilemma does not involve just a few players; it involves large numbers of groups. The costs and difficulties of organizing effective collective action — the constitutional revolution — that would defuse the dilemma, in such a context, cannot be over-emphasized. Nor, apparently, is there as yet much awareness on the part of the players of the situation that they are now in as regards this matter. Thus, there is another possible long-run outcome to this disastrous game that requires mention. It is not impossible that the workings of the capture process will intensify, and to such a point that some form of open despotism is the eventual outcome. Nevertheless, the prospect of constitutional revolution, before that time, cannot be entirely discounted.

The conclusion to the analysis here advanced is thus open-ended. There are a variety of paths that the unravelling system may take, according to the relative speeds and strengths of the various underlying processes involved. We cannot predict, with any certainty, where history will lead. But we may also certainly conclude on the matters at hand with the words of Henry Simons:

> . . . we should clearly sense the fact that minorities, industrial or functional minorities especially, are the great nemesis to democracy and that democracy, if it survives, must, above all, learn how to discipline and de-organize such minorities as special-interest pressure groups.[26]

NOTES

CHAPTER ONE

1. Henderson, (1979), p. 29.
2. Shenfield, (1974), p. 39.
3. Maddison, (1977).
4. Hutton, (1980), p. 8.
5. The perspective outlined in the Section is set out at much greater length in Burton (1984).
6. See Addison Chapter Two of this volume, and Burton (1984), for substantiation of this conclusion.
7. Phelps Brown, (1973), p. 334.
8. Johnson and Mieszkowski, (1970), p. 560.
9. See Burton, (1981).
10. Minford, (1981).

CHAPTER TWO

1. See Friedman, (1951), p. 222.
2. We note in parenthesis that Friedman would concede this point. Thus he would accept that the growth in the power of U.S. unions resulting from New Deal legislation was associated with wage push inflation (Friedman and Schwartz, 1963, p. 419). Again, such events are viewed as the exception rather than the rule.
3. See de Menil (1971), Johnston and Timbrell (1973).
4. That is, unions as transmitters of inflationary pressure behave in a manner that is mechanically different from the classical demand-supply adjustment process.
5. A second version of the militancy model has sociological roots, and is not separately examined here. For a discussion of this approach, however, see Addison and Burton (1982).
6. Actually, the ratio of unionized workers to the labour force.
7. Hines also employs a level of union density variable on the grounds that a unit increase in union density will have more effect on wage change at higher levels of unionization.

8. After Mulvey and Gregory (1977a) the arithmetically weighted wage level may be written:

$$W = (1 - T)W_n + TW_u \tag{1}$$

where W_n is the average nonunion wage
W_u is the average union wage
T is union density

Expressing the union-nonunion wage differential as

$$\lambda = \frac{W_u - W_n}{W_n} \ ,$$

the union wage may be written

$$W_u = W_n (1 + \lambda) \tag{2}$$

Substituting (2) into (1) yields

$$W = W_n (1 + T\lambda). \tag{3}$$

In order to identify the possible channels through which unions can cause the money wage level to change involves differentiating (3) with respect to time, to yield

$$\dot{W} = \dot{W}_n + [T/(1 + T\lambda)] \ \frac{\partial \lambda}{\partial t} + [\lambda(1 + T\lambda)] \ \frac{\partial T}{\partial t} \tag{4}$$

The three terms on the RHS of (4) respectively tell us that unions may cause wages to rise (a) by influencing the nonunion wage, (b) by increasing the union-nonunion differential, assuming union-nonunion employment is inelastic with respect to relative wages, and (c) by increasing union density.

9. On this point, see Burton (1972).
10. Cf. Godfrey (1971) and Ward and Zis (1974).
11. See, *inter al.*, Bain and Elsheik (1976), Richardson (1977), Shorey (1977).
12. See fn. 8.

13. Indirect in that the tests have focused on wage *settlements* while the model refers only to wage *claims*.
14. Cf. Hines (1969) and Sargan (1971).
15. See Eckstein and Wilson (1962) and Eckstein (1968).
16. See Ashenfelter, Johnson and Pencavel (1972).
17. Approximately 3 million British workers are covered by the (tripartite) wage councils whose (separate) rates once fixed are enforceable by the machinery of the criminal law.
18. Point (c) translates into a statement concerning the intercept term of the Phillips relation, while (b) relates to the slope of that function.
19. See, *inter al*. Wachter (1976), Riddell (1979), Mitchell (1980), and Christofides, Swidinsky and Wilton (1980b).
20. See Mitchell, (1980), table 4.3, p. 122.
21. The following analysis draws on Burton (1980).
22. Though the motivation of unions to push is unclear (see below).
23. See Brunner (1975).
24. The reasoning is that increases in the budget deficit will give rise to the acquisition by private agents of nominal debt which, while balanced formally by future tax liabilities, will nevertheless not represent a desired balance in their portfolios between financial assets, money and goods. Private agents, so the argument runs, will attempt to shift their portfolio composition back towards the desired balance, by adjusting their spending and swapping bonds for money. The effects of this extra demand (given the maintained hypothesis of inelastic supply) will be continually rising prices until the assets are held. The rise in inflation causes existing stocks of money assets fixed in money terms to fall in real terms. Consequently, holders need to acquire the additional assets injected by the government so as to restore their holding of assets to their equilibrium values. This portfolio balance effect means that a higher budget deficit yields higher inflation.
25. For a criticism of this procedure, see Sheehan and Grieves (1982).
26. Which constraint Borjas does not separately analyze.

CHAPTER THREE

1. For a comparative study of labour productivity in the British and continental automobile industries, see Central Policy Review Staff (1975).
2. Pratten acknowledges that he may have included a disproportionate number of international companies with relatively low productivity in the U.K.
3. Thus, for example, Caves uses certain combinations of variables that lead to difficulties in sampling theory. Hence his significance tests are in doubt. It is also unsatisfactory to enter the dependent variable as a ratio when measuring the independent variables in terms of absolute values, as does Caves. Problems of multicollinearity also attach to Caves' two independent variables, strikes and plant size. Moreover the assumed exogeneity of strikes is questionable: both inventories and strikes may be jointly determined by uncertainty. More generally, Caves' single equation approach is unsatisfactory.
4. Using the Harberger (1954) method, the value output loss of union monopoly is computed as half the product of the absolute wage and employment effects. Accordingly, the output loss depends upon the union-nonunion differential, the size of the union sector, and the elasticity of derived demand for labour in the union and nonunion sectors. Recent estimates point to a lower elasticity of derived demand in the union sector, and to this extent the above estimates are upwardly biased. Both Rees and Burton assume the elasticity to be unity in both sectors.
5. Here we refer to difficulties attaching to measurement of the aggregate union-nonunion differential, on which see Lewis (1981).
6. But note that for the public goods dimension of the workplace to be relevant two further conditions have to be met: there must be substantial search costs to using the 'market' for both firms and their workers *and* the firm needs to be subject to a number of imperfectly

foreseen changes in product market, technology, and other operating conditions. Both elements are recognized by Freeman (1976).

7. Freeman, (1976), p. 361.
8. Other variables, which vary according to the study, include the supervisor-labour ratio and size of establishment (to capture returns to scale).
9. For a fuller discussion, see Addison and Barnett (1982a,b).
10. These may be itemized as follows. First, the other studies (with the exception of Freeman, Connerton and Medoff, 1982) use value added as the dependent variable. This not only compounds price and productivity effects but also would seem simply to provide a measure of the union-nonunion differential by another route. Second, all other studies assume a similar production function across unionized and nonunionized firms. Third, no controls for 'firm effects' (e.g. superior management) are employed.
11. More accurately, Clark's results provide inadequate evidence to allow us to reject the (null) hypothesis that unionization has no effect on productivity.
12. The exception is the study by Brown and Medoff (1978), who attribute one-fifth of the union productivity effect to reduced turnover. Unfortunately, the authors' test procedures are flawed because they are unable to control for the stable worker.
13. See Duncan and Stafford (1980) for a theoretical and empirical amplification of this argument.
14. The problem alluded to here is that it is difficult to disentangle substitution and efficiency effects.
15. Both this coefficient and the one reported below are significant at conventional levels.
16. Harvard analysts in general and Freeman and Medoff (1979) in particular assume away as benign union activity in the political marketplace.
17. See Addison (1974).
18. See National Joint Advisory Council (1962).
19. Cf. Elliott (1980) and Brown and Terry (1978).
20. On these arguments, see Ulman (1968).
21. See Nelson (1981).

CHAPTER FOUR

1. Quoted in Brittan, (1977), p. 121.
2. Thompson, (1979), p. 36.
3. Reflecting the German situation, von Weizsäcker assumes the presence of a strong central bank, independent of the executive.
4. The basic argument here is that society can be regulated by economic means only to the extent that social action takes a form amenable to incorporation in market transactions.
5. Brittan, (1977), p. 123.
6. This stipulated a flat rate increase of 6 pounds per week for the year to August 1976. Those earning in excess of 8,500 pounds per year were to get nothing. These and other details are documented in Fallick and Elliott 1981, pp. 264-275.
7. Pay increases of 5 per cent were stipulated, subject to upper and lower limits of 4 pounds and 2.25 pounds per week respectively.
8. *Winning the Battle Against Inflation*, Cmnd. 7293.
9. In addition, The Employment Protection Act (EPA) of 1975 augmented somewhat the powers granted to the unions under the Trade Unions and Labour Relations Act of 1974. Thus it obliged employers to disclose company information to representatives of recognized unions where this was "required" for purposes of collective bargaining. Also, employees were protected from dismissal for joining a trade union — no such protection was extended those dismissed for *refusing* to join a union. Again, the ease of obtaining union recognition as official bargaining agent, and the ease of negotiating a closed shop agreement, were increased in theory by the establishment and terms of reference of two statutory bodies under the EPA, namely the Advisory, Conciliation and Arbitration Service and the Central Arbitration Committee. Little comment is required on these two agencies since the problematic clause was excised by the 1980 Employment Act.
10. Bullock, (1977), p.v.
11. The distinction between the two is worth preserving for

analytical purposes. Thus, for example, one might argue that the closed shop legislation was more geared to the interests of the leadership than the membership, as does Burton (Chapter Six), even though that legislation shifted the Marshallian conditions in a manner favourable to the membership.

12. On the free-rider issue, however, see Bennett and Johnson (1980).
13. On which see Chiplin, Coyne and Sirc (1977).
14. The 1971 Act contained eight basic principles: the statutory right to belong or not to belong to a union; the establishment of an official Register of trade unions and employers' associations; the limitation of legal immunities for unregistered unions; the potential for legally-enforceable collective agreements; a minor redefinition of legal picketing; recognition rights for trade unions; machinery to define bargaining representation within work units; the selective enforcement of industrial relations procedure agreements; and emergency provision for the Secretary of State to apply to a new Industrial Relations Court for a cooling-off period of 60 days, or for compulsory ballots, under certain specified conditions.
15. See Addison (1982).
16. Hibbs' model employs a real wage hypothesis, where the expectation-achievement function is one of long-run expectations with a polynomial distributed lag.
17. Crouch, (1978), p. 224.

CHAPTER FIVE

1. *Industrial Democracy*, London: HMSO, 1978. For an economic evaluation of this legislative proposal see Addison (1980).
2. Mr. Tony Benn, perhaps Britain's most influential left-wing politician, is a redoubtable advocate of "industrial democracy."
3. M. Dobbs, 'Solidarity Asks Party for Vote,' Washington Post, September 9, 1981, p. Al.
4. Vanek, (1971), pp. 8-12.
5. There have been some important changes in the details

of the Yugoslavian system since the mid-1970s. See Moore (1981) for a summary and economic analysis of the implications of these changes.

6. One distinguishing feature of the Mondragon co-operatives is that voting in worker general assemblies is allocated not on a "one man, one vote" principle but in rough accordance with relative wages. 'Thus an assembly-line worker might have one or two votes, compared with three votes for the tiny minority paid at the top rate' (Oakeshott, 1975, p. 292). See also Johnson and Whyte (1977), on the details of the Mondragon system.

7. The *ceteris paribus* clause is significant here. The more even is the balance of voting strength as between alternative policies, the greater is the influence of the individual voter/member on the outcome.

8. The ability of a dominant coalition in a market syndicalist enterprise to "exploit" minorities in the workforce in this way will depend upon the possibilities of exit to alternative job opportunities. This matter is taken up later.

9. Lindblom, (1949), Chapter XVI.

10. Vanek, (1971), p. 38.

11. Jay allows that the U.S.A. may possibly escape the disease without resort to the radical property rights restructuring that he proposes.

12. Jay, (1976), p. 23.

13. *Ibid*. p. 27.

14. The argument in the sections on "Market Syndicalism and the Problem of Producer Group Power" and "Market Syndicalism and the British Disease" draws upon Burton (1983).

15. Even the advocates of market syndicalism have been much troubled by this point. For example, Vanek (1975b, p. 446) states that 'it had always puzzled me how it could have been possible that a productive organization based on co-operation, harmony of interests and the brotherhood of man, so appealing and desirable on moral and philosophical grounds, could have done so poorly when subjected to a practical test.'

16. Vanek, (1970), p. 244.

17. O'Mahoney, (1979), p. 31.
18. Bajt, 1968, p. 3.
19. The implications of the 1976 legislation are examined in detail by Moore (1980).
20. The difficulties of grafting on entrepreneurship to a market syndicalist economy are considered at length by O'Mahoney (1979).
21. Cole, (1920a), pp. 27-29.
22. Connock, (1973), p. 9.
23. As Vanek (1972, ch. 4) notes, 'the liquidation of enterprises [in Yugoslavia] is exceptional and usually only occurs in the case of minor shops or workshops with little or no capital resources.'
24. This possibility was intimated first by Meade (1972).
25. See the discussion on this matter in the chapter on Trade Unionism and the British Disease previously.
26. Congdon, (1975), p. 256.

CHAPTER SIX

1. An analysis that emphasizes some similar themes has earlier been forwarded by Olson (1982).
2. All page references here given refer to the 1980 source.
3. Simons, (1980), p. 2.
4. *Ibid*., p. 8.
5. *Ibid*., p. 7.
6. *Ibid*., p. 4.
7. *Ibid*., p. 4.
8. The term "prisoner's dilemma" arises from consideration of the decision problems facing a criminal gang that have been arrested, and interrogated separately. If no one cracks during interrogation — if no one confesses — then they are all likely to get off with a light (or zero) sentence. If only one confesses, then he is likely to get off relatively lightly, while the others are handed down more severe sentences. If all confess, they will all get sentenced, but less severely than in the latter case. Thus the incentive is, in this dilemma situation (to confess or not to confess), for each rational decision-maker to confess, hoping no one else will. But all (acting rationally and in the pursuit of self-interest) will do this. The

general outcome is thus worse for all than if they had been able to make a binding agreement among themselves that no one will confess to the crime.

9. Simons (1980, p. 22) conclusion on this matter was that there could be no absolute freedom of association, for any purposes: '. . . the right of voluntary association must always be qualified, *inter alia*, by prohibitions against monopolizing. . .'

10. *Ibid.*, p. 15.

11. See Parsley (1980) for a survey of evidence on the relative wage effects of unionism.

12. Addison (1982b), p. 7.

13. Freeman and Medoff, (1979).

14. See Reynolds (1981).

15. See also Addison on Trade Unions and Productivity in this volume.

16. Simons, (1980), p. 9.

17. The analysis of the operation of the exit and voice mechanisms within trade unions that follows is taken from Burton (1983).

18. The matter is analyzed in greater detail in Burton (1982).

19. See Bennett and Johnson (1981), p. 184.

20. Pencavel, (1977), p. 140.

21. Freeman and Medoff, (1982), p. 5.

22. Simons, (1980), p. 4.

23. For further commentary on this analysis see Burton (1980).

24. Freeman and Medoff, (1979), pp. 36-37.

25. The political influence of British unionism is detailed in Burton (1979).

26. Simons, (1980), p. 21.

REFERENCES

CHAPTER ONE

1. Alchian, A.A. (1950), 'Uncertainty, Evolution and Economic Theory,' *Journal of Political Economy*, Vol. LVIII, pp. 211-221.
2. Allen, G.C. (1979), *The British Disease*, London: Institute of Economic Affairs, 2nd ed.
3. Atkinson, A.B. and Flemming, J.S. (1978), 'Unemployment, Social Security and Incentives,' *Midland Bank Review*, Autumn, pp. 6-16.
4. Bacon, R. and Eltis, W. (1978), *Britain's Economic Problems: Too Few Producers*, London: Macmillan, 2nd ed.
5. Bailey, M.J. (1956), 'The Welfare Cost of Inflationary Finance,' *Journal of Political Economy*, Vol. 64, No. 2, pp. 93-110.
6. Bloch, F.E. (1980), 'Political Support for Minimum Wage Legislation,' *Journal of Labor Research*, Vol. 1, No. 2, Fall, pp. 245-253.
7. Brittan, S. (1978), 'How British is the British Sickness?,' *Journal of Law and Economics*, Vol. XXI, No. 2, Oct., pp. 245-268.
8. Buchanan, J.M. and Wagner, R.E. (1977), *Democracy in Deficit*, New York: Academic Press.
9. Burton, J. (1978), 'Are Trade Unions a Public Good/Bad?: The Economics of the Closed Shop,' in Robbins, L. (et al.), *Trade Unions: Public Goods or Public 'Bads'?* London: Institute of Economic Affairs, Readings 17, pp. 31-52.
10. Burton, J. (1979a), *The Job-Support Machine: A Critique of the Subsidy Morass*, London: Centre for Policy Studies.
11. Burton, J. (1979b), *The Trojan Horse: Union Power in British Politics*, London: Adam Smith Institute.
12. Burton, J. (1980a), 'The Demand for Inflation in Liberal Democratic Societies,' in P. Whiteley (ed.), *Models of Political Economy*, Beverly Hills: Sage Publications, pp. 221-248.

13. Burton, J. (1980b), 'Unionism, Inflation and Unemployment,' *Vie et Sciences Economiques*, Juillet, No. 86, (Numéro Spécial: L'Economie des Syndicats), pp. 37-48.
14. Burton, J. (1980c), 'The Political Economy of Free Collective Chaos,' *Focus*, Vol. I, No. 1, pp. 1-11.
15. Burton, J. (1980d), 'Trade Unions' Role in the British Disease: An Interest in Inflation?,' in P. Minford et al., *Is Monetarism Enough?*, London: Institute of Economic Affairs, pp. 99-111.
16. Burton, J. (1981), 'The Thatcher Experiment: A Requiem?,' *Journal of Labor Research*, Vol. II, August, Research Monograph I.
17. Burton, J. (1984), *Trade Unions, Stagflation, and Economic Policy*, London: Macmillan, forthcoming.
18. Downs, D. (1957), *An Economic Theory of Democracy*, New York: Harper and Row.
19. Friedman, M. (1951), 'Some Comments on the Significance of Labor Unions for Economic Policy,' in Wright, D.M. (ed.), *The Impact of the Union*, New York: Harcourt Brace, pp. 204-234.
20. Friedman, M. (1977), 'Nobel Lecture: Inflation and Unemployment,' *Journal of Political Economy*, Vol. 85, No. 3, pp. 451-472.
21. Gordon, D.F. (1975), 'The Demand For and Supply Of Inflation,' *Journal of Law and Economics*, Vol. XVIII, No. 3, Dec., pp. 807-836.
22. Hayek, F.A. (1958), 'Unions, Inflation, and Profits,' in Bradley, P.D. (ed.), *The Public Stake in Union Power*, Charlottesville: University of Virginia Press, pp. 46-62.
23. Hayek, F.A. (1960), *The Constitution of Liberty*, London: Routledge and Kegan Paul.
24. Henderson, N. (1979), 'Britain's Decline; Its Causes and Consequences,' *The Economist*, June 2, pp. 29-40.
25. Hicks, John R., *Crisis in Keynesian Economics*, London, Blackwell, 1974.
26. Hutton, G. (1980), *Whatever Happened to Productivity?*, London: Institute of Economic Affairs.
27. Johnson, H.G. and Mieszkowski, P. (1970), 'The Effects of Unionization on the Distribution of Income: A General Equilibrium Approach,' *Quarterly Journal of Economics*, Vol. LXXXIV, No. 3, June, pp. 509-561.

28. Joseph, K. (1979), *Solving the Union Problem is the Key to Britain's Recovery*, London: Centre for Policy Studies.
29. Kahn, Lord, *On Rereading Lord Keynes*, London, British Academy, 1975.
30. Kaldor, N. (1966), *Causes of the Slow Rate of Growth in the U.K.*, Cambridge.
31. Knapp, J. (1968), 'Pragmatism and the British Malaise,' *LLoyds Bank Review*, No. 90, pp. 1-21.
32. Layard, R., Metcalf, D. and Nickell, S. (1977), 'The Effect of Collective Bargaining on Wages,' London School of Economics: Centre for Labour Economics (mimeo).
33. Maddison, A. (1977), 'Phases of Capitalist Development,' *Banca Nazionale del Lavoro Quarterly Review*, No. 121, June, pp. 103-137.
34. Minford, P. (1981), *The Problem of Unemployment*, London: Selsdon Group Policy Series.
35. Olson, M. (1982), *The Rise and Decline of Nations: Economic Growth, Stagflation, and Social Rigidities*, New Haven, Conn.: Yale University Press.
36. Paige, D.C. (1961), 'Economic Growth: The Last Hundred Years,' *National Institute Economic Review*, July, pp. 24-49.
37. Pencavel, J.H. (1977), 'The Distribution and Efficiency Effects of Trade Unions in Britain,' *British Journal of Industrial Relations*, Vol. 15, No. 2, July, pp. 137-156.
38. Phelps Brown, E.H. (1973), 'New Wine in Old Bottles: Reflections on the Changed Working of Collective Bargaining,' *British Journal of Industrial Relations*, Vol. XI, No. 3, Nov., pp. 329-337.
39. Rees, A. (1963), 'The Effects of Unions on Resource Allocation,' *Journal of Law and Economics*, Vol. 6, Oct., pp. 69-78.
40. Shenfield, A. (1974), 'The English Disease,' *Moorgate and Wall Street Review*, Autumn, pp. 39-60.
41. Stigler, G.J. (1971), 'The Theory of Economic Regulation,' *Bell Journal of Economics and Management Science*, Vol. 2, No. 1, Spring, pp. 3-21.
42. Stillman, E., et al., (1974), *The United Kingdom in 1980*, London Associated Business Programmes.
43. Thomas, R.L. (1977), 'Unionisation and the Phillips

Curve — Time Series Evidence from Seven Industrialised Countries,' *Applied Economics*, Vol. 9, No. 1, March, pp. 33-49.
44. Willett, T.D. and Laney, L.O. (1978), 'Monetarism, Budget Deficits and Wage Push Inflation: The Cases of Italy and the U.K.,' *Banca Nazionale del Lavoro Quarterly Review*, No. 127, Dec., pp. 315-331.

CHAPTER TWO

1. Addison, J.T. and Burton, J. (1982), "The Sociopolitical Analysis of Inflation," *mimeographed*, University of South Carolina.
2. Ashenfelter, O.C., Johnson, G.E. and Pencavel, J.H. (1972), "Trade Unions and the Rate of Change of Money Wages in United States Manufacturing Industry," *Review of Economic Studies*, Vol. 39, No. 117, January, pp. 27-54.
3. Bain, G.S. and Elsheik, F. (1976), *Union Growth and the Business Cycle*, London: Basil Blackwell.
4. Beenstock, M. and Immanuel, H. (1979), "The Market Approach to Pay Comparability," *National Westminister Bank Review*, November, pp. 26-41.
5. Borjas, G.J. (1980), "Wage Determination in the Federal Government: The Role of Constituents and Bureaucrats," *Journal of Political Economy*, Vol. 88, No. 6, December, pp. 1110-1147.
6. Brennan, G. and Buchanan, J.M. (1977), "Toward a Tax Constitution for Leviathan," *Journal of Public Economics*, Vol. 8, No. 3, December, pp. 255-273.
7. Brunner, K. (1975), "Comment [on Gordon]," *Journal of Law and Economics*, Vol. 18, No. 3, December, pp. 837-857.
8. Burton, J. (1972), *Wage Inflation*, London: Macmillan.
9. Burton, J. (1980), "Unionism, Inflation and Unemployment," *Vie et Sciences Economiques*, No. 86, Juillet, pp. 37-48.
10. Burton, J. (1984), *Trade Unions, Stagflation, and Economic Policy*, London: Macmillan (forthcoming).
11. Burton, J. and Addison, J.T. (1977), "The Institutionalist Analysis of Wage Inflation: A Critical Apprais-

al," *Research in Labor Economics*, Vol. 1, No. 1, pp. 333-376.

12. Chester, E. (1977), "Some Social and Economic Determinants of Non-Military Public Spending," *Public Finance*, Vol. 32, No. 2, July, pp. 451-469.

13. Christofides, L.N., Swidinsky, R. and Wilton, D.A. (1980a), "A Microeconometric Analysis of Spillover within the Canadian Wage Determination Process," *Review of Economics and Statistics*, Vol. 52, No. 2, May, pp. 213-221.

14. Christofides, L.N., Swidinsky, R. and Wilton, D.A. (1980b), "A Microeconometric Analysis of the Canadian Wage Determination Process," *Economica*, Vol. 47, No. 186, May, pp. 165-178.

15. de Menil, G. (1971), *Bargaining: Monopoly Power – Versus Union Power*, Cambridge, Mass.: MIT Press.

16. Dudley, L. and Montmarquette, C. (1982), "The Median Voter Versus Leviathan: Tests of Alternative Models of Public Spending," *mimeographed*, University of Montreal.

17. Eckstein, O. and Wilson, R.A. (1962), "The Determination of Money Wages in American Industry," *Quarterly Journal of Economics*, Vol. 76, No. 3, August, pp. 379-414.

18. Eckstein, O. (1968), "Money Wage Determination Revisited," *Review of Economic Studies*, Vol. 35, No. 102, January, pp. 133-143.

19. Elliott, R.F. (1976), "The National Wage Round in the U.K.: A Sceptical View," *Oxford Bulletin*, Vol. 38, No. 3, August, pp. 179-201.

20. Fallick, J.L. and Elliott, R.F. (1981), "Incomes Policy and the Public Sector," in Fallick and Elliott (eds.), *Incomes Policies, Inflation and Relative Pay*, London: George Allen and Unwin, pp. 100-127.

21. Flanagan, R.J. (1976), "Wage Interdependence in Unionized Labor Markets," *Brookings Papers on Economic Activity*, No. 3, pp. 635-673.

22. Friedman, M. (1951), "Some Comments on the Significance of Labor Unions for Economic Policy," in Wright, D.M. (ed.), *The Impact of the Union*, New York: Harcourt Brace, pp. 204-234.

23. Friedman, M. (1970), *The Counter-Revolution in Monetary Theory*, London: Institute of Economic Affairs.
24. Friedman, M. and Schwartz, A.J. (1963), *A Monetary History of the United States 1867-1960*, Princeton, N.J.: Princeton University Press.
25. Godfrey, L. (1971), "The Phillips Curve: Incomes Policy and Trade Union Effects," in Johnson and Nobay (eds.), *op cit.*, pp. 99-124.
26. Gordon, R.J. (1975), "The Demand for and Supply of Inflation," *Journal of Law and Economics*, Vol. 18, No. 3, December, pp. 807-836.
27. Gordon, R.J. (1977), "World Inflation and Monetary Accommodation in Eight Countries," *Brookings Papers on Economic Activity*, No. 2, pp. 409-468.
28. Hayek, F.A. (1958), "Unions, Inflation, and Profits," Bradley, P.D. (Ed.), *The Public Stake in Union Power*, Charlottesville, Virginia: University of Virginia Press, pp. 46-62.
29. Hines, A.G. (1964), "Trade Unions and Wage Inflation in the United Kingdom, 1893-1961," *Review of Economic Studies*, Vol. 31, No. 2, October, pp. 221-252.
30. Hines, A.G. (1968), "Unemployment and the Rate of Change of Money Wage Rates in the United Kingdom, 1962-1963: A Reappraisal," *Review of Economics and Statistics*, Vol. 50, No. 1, February, pp. 60-67.
31. Hines, A.G. (1969), "Wage Inflation in the United Kingdom, 1948-62: A Disaggregated Study," *Economic Journal*, Vol. 79, No. 313, March, pp. 66-89.
32. Hines, A.G. (1971), "The Determinants of the Rate of Change of Money Wage Rates and the Effectiveness of Incomes Policy," in Johnson and Nobay (eds.), *op. cit.*, pp. 143-175.
33. Johnson, H.G. and Nobay, A.R. (eds.) (1971), *The Current Inflation*, London: Macmillan.
34. Johnston, J. (1972), "A Model of Wage Determination under Bilateral Monopoly," *Economic Journal*, Vol. 82, No. 327, September, pp. 837-852.
35. Johnston, J. and Timbrell, M. (1973), "Empirical Tests of a Bargaining Theory of Wage Rate Determination," *Manchester School*, Vol. 41, No. 2, June, pp. 161-167.
36. Kahn, R. (1976), "Inflation — A Keynesian View,"

Scottish Journal of Political Economy, Vol. 23, No. 1, February, pp. 11-16.

37. Knowles, K.G.J.C. and Thorne, E.M. (1961), "Wage Rounds 1948-59," *Oxford Bulletin*, Vol. 23, No. 1, February, pp. 1-26.

38. Knowles, K.G.J.C. and Robinson, D. (1962), "Wage Rounds and Wage Policy," *Oxford Bulletin*, Vol. 24, No. 2, May, pp. 269-329.

39. Layard, R., Metcalf, D. and Nickell, S. (1978), "The Effect of Collective Bargaining on Relative and Absolute Wages," *British Journal of Industrial Relations*, Vol. 16, No. 3, November, pp. 287-302.

40. Mitchell, D.J.B. (1980), *Unions, Wages and Inflation*, Washington, D.C.: The Brookings Institution.

41. Minford, P. (1980), "Monetarism, Inflation and Economic Policy," in *Is Monetarism Enough?*, IEA Readings 24, London: Institute of Economic Affairs, pp. 3-23.

42. Mulvey, C. (1978), "Unions, Spillovers and Relative Wages," *Working Paper No. 111*, Industrial Relations Section, Princeton University, March.

43. Mulvey, C. and Gregory, M. (1977a), "The Hines Wage Inflation Model," *Manchester School*, Vol. 45, No. 1, March, pp. 29-40.

44. Mulvey, C. and Gregory, M. (1977b), "Trade Unions and Inflation in the U.K. — An Exercise," Discussion Paper in Economics No. 22, University of Glasgow.

45. Parkin, J.M.(1977), "Comments and Discussion [on Gordon]" *Brookings Papers on Economic Activity*, No. 2, pp. 471-474.

46. Peacock, A.T. and Ricketts, M. (1978), "The Growth of the Public Sector and Inflation," in Hirsch, F. and Goldthorpe, J.H. (eds.), *The Politial Economy of Inflation*, London: Martin Robertson, pp. 117-136.

47. Richardson, R. (1977), "Trade Union Growth," *British Journal of Industrial Relations*, Vol. 15, No. 2, July, pp. 279-282.

48. Riddel, W.C., (1979), "The Empirical Foundations of the Phillips Curve: Evidence for Canadian Wage Contract Data," *Econometrica*, Vol. 47, No. 1, June, pp. 1-24.

49. Sargan, J.D. (1971), "A Study of Wages and Prices in the U.K. 1949-1968," in Johnson and Nobay (eds.), *op. cit.*

50. Sheehan, R.G. and Grieves, R. (1982), "Sunspots and Cycles: A Test of Causation," *Southern Economic Journal*, Vol. 48, No. 3, January, pp. 775-777.

51. Shorey, J. (1977), "Time-Series Analysis of Strike Frequency," *British Journal of Industrial Relations*, Vol. 15, No. 2, July, pp. 63-75.

52. Steele, R. (1979), "The Relative Performance of the Wages Council and Non-Wages Council Sectors and the Impact of Incomes Policy," *British Journal of Industrial Relations*, Vol. 17, No. 2, July, pp. 224-234.

53. Swidinsky, R. (1972), "Trade Unions and the Rate of Change of Money Wages in Canada," 1953-1976, *Industrial and Labor Relations Review*, Vol. 25, No. 3, April, pp. 363-375.

54. Wachter, M.L. (1974), "The Wage Process: An Analysis of the Early 1970s," *Brookings Papers on Economic Activity*, No. 2, pp. 507-524.

55. Wachter, M.L. (1976), "The Changing Cyclical Responsiveness of Wage Inflation," *Brookings Papers on Economic Activity*, No. 2, pp. 115-167.

56. Ward, K. and Zis, G. (1974), "Trade Union Militancy as an Explanation of Inflation: An International Comparison," *Manchester School*, Vol. 42, No. 1, March, pp. 46-65.

57. Willett, T.D. and Laney, L.O. (1978), "Monetarism, Budget Deficits, and Wage Push Inflation: The Cases of Italy and the U.K.," *Banca Nazionale del Lavoro Quarterly Review*, No. 127, December, pp. 315-331.

58. Wilkinson, R.K. and Burkitt, B. (1973), "Wage Determination and Trade Unions," *Scottish Journal of Political Economy*, Vol. 20, No. 2, June, pp. 107-122.

CHAPTER THREE

1. Addison, J.T. (1974), "Productivity Bargaining: The Externalities Question," *Scottish Journal of Political Economy*, Vol. 21, No. 2, June, pp. 122-142.

2. Addison, J.T. (1981), "Trade Unions and Restrictive

Practices," in Rosa, J.J. (ed.), *The Economics of Labor Unions*, Amsterdam: Kluwer-Nijhoff.

3. Addison, J.T. and Barnett, A.H. (1983a), "The Impact of Unionization on Productivity," *British Journal of Industrial Relations*, Vol. 20, No. 2, July, pp. 145-162.

4. Addison, J.T. and Barnett, A.H. (1981b), "Unionization and Productivity," *mimeographed*, Department of Economics, University of South Carolina.

5. Allen, S.G. (1979), *Unionized Construction Workers Are More Productive*, Washington, D.C.: Center to Protect Workers' Rights, November.

6. British Iron and Steel Federation (1967), *Labour Productivity in the Steel Industry*.

7. Brown, W. and Terry, M. (1978), "The Changing Nature of National Wage Agreements," *Scottish Journal of Political Economy*, Vol. 25, No. 2, June, pp. 119-133.

8. Brown, C. and Medoff, J.L. (1978), "Trade Unions in the Production Process," *Journal of Political Economy*, Vol. 86, No. 3, June, pp. 355-378.

9. Burton, J. (1978), "Are Trade Unions a Public Good/ Bad?: The Economics of the Closed Shop," in *Trade Unions – Public Goods or Public 'Bads'?* IEA Readings 17, London: Institute of Economic Affairs.

10. Caves, R.E. (1980), "Productivity Differences Among Industries," in Caves, R.E. and Krause, L.B. (eds.), *Britain's Economic Performance*, Washington, D.C.: The Brookings Institution, pp. 135-192.

11. Central Policy Review Staff (1975), *The Future of the British Car Industry*, London: HMSO.

12. Clark, K.B. (1980a), "The Impact of Unionization of Productivity: A Case Study," *Industrial and Labor Relations Review*, Vol. 33, No. 4, July, pp. 451-469.

13. Clark, K.B. (1980b), "Unionization and Productivity: Micro-Econometric Evidence," *Quarterly Journal of Economics*, Vol. 95, No. 4, December, pp. 613-639.

14. Clark, K.B. (1982), "Unionization and Firm Performance: The Impact of Profits, Growth and Productivity," *Working Paper HBS 83-16*, Harvard University.

15. Donovan (1968), Royal Commission on Trade Unions and Employers' Associations, *Report*, London: HMSO, Cmnd. 3623.

16. Duncan, G.J. and Stafford, F.P. (1980), "Do Union Members Receive Compensating Differentials?" *American Economic Review*, Vol. 70, No. 3, June, pp. 355-371.
17. Elliott, R.F. (1980), "Are National Agreements Dead?" *Discussion Paper No. 80:13*, University of Aberdeen.
18. Flanders, A. (1964), *The Fawley Productivity Agreements*, London: Faber and Faber.
19. Frantz, J.R. (1976), 'The Impact of Trade Unions on Production in the Wooden Household Furniture Industry,' Senior Honors Thesis, Harvard University, March.
20. Freeman, R.B. (1976), "Individual Mobility and Union Voice in the Labor Market," *American Economic Review, Papers and Proceedings*, Vol. 66, No. 2, May, pp. 361-368.
21. Freeman, R.B. and Medoff, J.L. (1979), "The Two Faces of Unionism," *Public Interest*, Fall, pp. 69-93.
22. Freeman, R.B., Medoff, J.L. and Connerton, M.L. (1982), "Industrial Relations and Productivity: A Study of the U.S. Bituminous Coal Industry" (in process).
23. Harberger, A. (1954), "Monopoly and Resource Allocation," *American Economic Review, Papers and Proceedings*, Vol. 24, No. 2, May, pp. 77-87.
24. Hirsch, B. and Link, A.N. (1983), "Unions, Productivity and Productivity Growth," *mimeographed*, Journal of Labor Research (forthcoming).
25. Lewis, H.G. (1981), "Interpreting Unionism Coefficients in Wage Equations," *mimeographed*, Duke University.
26. Link, A.N. (1981), "Basic Research and Productivity Increase in Manufacturing: Some Additional Evidence," *American Economic Review*, Vol. 71, No. 5, December, pp. 1111-1112.
27. Maddison, A. (1977), "Phases of Capitalist Development," *Banca Nazionale del Lavoro Quarterly Review*, No. 121, June, pp. 103-137.
28. Mansfield, E. (1980), "Basic Research and Productivity Increase in Manufacturing," *American Economic Review*, Vol. 70, No. 5, December, pp. 863-973.
29. National Joint Advisory Council (1962), *Report of the*

Working Party on the Manpower Situation, Ministry of Labour Gazette, February, pp. 45-48.

30. NEDO (1967), *Manpower in the Chemical Industry: A Comparison of British and American Practices*, London: HMSO.

31. Nelson, R.N. (1981), "Research on Productivity Growth Differences," *Journal of Economic Literature*, Vol. 19, No. 3, September, pp. 1029-1064.

32. Olson, M. (1978), "The Political Economy of Comparative Growth Rates," *mimeographed*, University of Maryland.

33. Pencavel, J.H. (1977), "The Distributional and Efficiency Effects of Trade Unions in Britain," *British Journal of Industrial Relations*, Vol. 15, No. 2, July, pp. 137-156.

34. Pratten, C.F. (1976), *Labour Productivity Differences Within International Companies*, Cambridge: Cambridge University Press.

35. Phelps Brown, E.H. and Browne, M.H. (1968), *A Century of Pay: The Course of Pay and Production in France, Germany, Sweden, the United Kingdom, and the United States of America, 1860-1960*, London: Macmillan.

36. Ray, G.F. (1966), "The Size of Plant: A Comparison," *National Institute Economic Review*, No. 38, November, pp. 64-66.

37. Rees, A. (1963), "Effects of Unions on Resource Allocation," *Journal of Law and Economics*, Vol. 6, October, pp. 69-78.

38. Robinson, D. (1972), "Productivity Bargaining and Municipalities," *L.M.R.S. Newsletter*, Vol. 3, No. 8, August.

39. Rostas, L. (1948), *Comparative Productivity in British and American Industry*, National Institute of Economic and Social Research, Occasional Paper 13, Cambridge: Cambridge University Press.

40. Terleckyj, N.E. (1980), "What Do R & D Numbers Tell Us About Technological Change?" *American Economic Review, Papers and Proceedings*, Vol. 70, No. 2, May, pp. 55-61.

41. Ulman, L. (1968), "Collective Bargaining and Indus-

trial Efficiency," in Caves, R.E. *et al.*, *Britain's Economic Prospects*, London: George Allen and Unwin, pp. 324-380.

CHAPTER FOUR

1. Addison, J.T. (1982), "Trades Unions, Corporatism and Inflation," *mimeographed*, University of South Carolina.
2. Akerlof, G.A. (1978), "A Theory of Social Custom of Which Unemployment May Be One Consequence," Special Studies Paper No. 118, Board of Governors of the Federal Reserve System.
3. Alchian, A.A. (1951), "Uncertainty, Evolution and Economic Theory," *Journal of Political Economy*, Vol. 58, No. 3, June, pp. 211-221.
4. Bennett, J. and Johnson, M. (1980), "Free Riders in U.S. Labor Unions: Artifice or Affliction?" *British Journal of Industrial Relations*, Vol. 28, No. 2, July, pp. 158-172.
5. Braun, A.R. (1978), *Incomes Policies in Industrial Countries Since 1973*, DM/78/8, Washington, D.C.: International Monetary Fund.
6. Brittan, S. (1977), *The Economic Consequences of Democracy*, London: Temple Smith.
7. Bullock (1977), *Report of the Committee of Inquiry on Industrial Democracy*, London: H.M.S.O. Cmnd. 6706.
8. Chiplin, B., Coyne, J. and Sirc, L. (1977), *Can Workers Manage,?* Hobart Paper 77, London: Institute of Economic Affairs.
9. Crouch, C.J. (1978), "Inflation and the Political Organisation of Economic Interests," in Hirsch, F. and Goldthorpe, J.H. (eds.), *The Political Economy of Inflation*, London: Martin Robertson, pp. 217-239.
10. Crouch, C.J. (1983), "The Conditions for Trade Union Wage Restraint," in Lindberg, L. and Maier, C. (eds.), *The Politics and Sociology of Global Inflation*, Washington, D.C.: The Brookings Institution (forthcoming).
11. Davies, R.J. (1983), "The Political Economy of Strikes: An Empirical Analysis of the Group of Ten," in Rosa,

J-J ed., *The Economics of Labour Unions*, Amsterdam; Kluwer Nijhoff (forthcoming).
12. Dicey, A.V. (1914), *Lectures on the Relation Between Law and Public Opinion in England During the Nineteenth Century*, London: Macmillan.
13. Dicey, A.V. (1963), *Law and Public Opinion in England*, London: Macmillan, 2nd edition.
14. Fallick, J.L. and Elliott, R.S., eds. (1981), *Incomes Policy, Inflation and Relative Pay*, London: George Allen and Unwin.
15. Galbraith, J.K. (1967), *The New Industrial State*, New York: Houghton Mifflin.
16. Gennard, J., Dunn, S. and Wright, M. (1979), "The Content of British Closed Shop Agreements," *Department of Employment Gazette*, November.
17. Gennard, J., Dunn, S. and Wright, M. (1980), "The Extent of Closed Shop Arrangements in British Industry," *Department of Employment Gazette*, January.
18. Hanson, C., Jackson, S. and Miller, D. (1982), *The Closed Shop*, New York: St. Martins Press.
19. Hibbs, D.A. (1976), "Industrial Conflict in Advanced Industrial Societies," *American Political Science Review*, Vol. 70, No. 4, December, pp. 1033-1058.
20. Hibbs, D.A. (1977), "Political Parties and Macroeconomic Policy," *American Political Science Review*, Vol. 71, No. 4, December, pp. 1467-1487.
21. Hibbs, D.A. (1978), "On the Political Economy of Long-Run Trends in Strike Activity," *British Journal of Political Science*, Vol. 8, No. 2, April, pp. 153-175.
22. Katona, G. *et al.* (1971), *Aspirations and Affluence*, New York: McGraw-Hill.
23. Layard, R., Metcalf, D. and Nickell, S. (1978), "The Effect of Collective Bargaining on Relative and Absolute Wages," *British Journal of Industrial Relations*, Vol. 16, No. 3, November, pp. 287-302.
24. McCarthy, W.E.J. (1964), *The Closed Shop in Britain*, Oxford: Basil Blackwell.
25. Minford, P. (1981), "Labour Market Equilibrium in an Open Economy," *Working Paper No. 8103*, University of Liverpool.
26. Myrdal, H.G. (1980), "The Swedish Model — Will It

Survive?," *British Journal of Industrial Relations*, Vol. 18, No. 1, March, pp. 57-69.

27. Nickell, S.J. (1980), "The Determinants of Equilibrium Unemployment in Britain," *Discussion Paper No. 78*, Centre for Labor Economics, London School of Economics.

28. Olson, M. (1978), "The Political Economy of Comparative Growth Rates," *mimeographed*, University of Maryland.

29. Scott, M. (1980), "The Cambridge Economic Policy Group's Case for Import Restrictions," in *The Arguments For and Against Protectionism*, Paper No. 19, London: Bank of England.

30. Siebert, W.S. and Addison, J.T. (1981), "Are Strikes Accidental?" *Economic Journal*, Vol. 91, No. 362, June, pp. 389-404.

31. Simons, H.C. (1944), "Some Reflections on Syndicalism," *Journal of Political Economy*, Vol. 44, No. 1, March, pp. 1-19.

32. Tobin, J. (1972), "Inflation and Unemployment," *American Economic Review*, Vol. 62, No. 1, March, pp. 1-18.

33. Thomson, A.W.J. (1979), "Trade Unions and the Corporate State in Britain," *Industrial and Labor Relations Review*, Vol. 33, No. 1, October, pp. 36-54.

34. Trevithick, J.A. (1976a), "Inflation, the Natural Unemployment Rate and the Theory of Economic Policy," *Scottish Journal of Political Economy*, Vol. 23, No. 1, February, pp. 37-53.

35. Trevithick, J.A. (1976b), "Money Wage Inflexibility and the Keynesian Labour Supply Function," *Economic Journal*, Vol. 86, No. 342, June, pp. 327-332.

36. Weizsäcker von, C.C. (1977), "The Employment Problem: A Systems Approach," *mimeographed*, Paris: OECD, March.

CHAPTER FIVE

1. Addison, J.T. (1980), 'Wither Industrial Democracy,' University of Aberdeen (mimeo).

2. Alchian, A. (1951), 'Uncertainty, Evolution and Eco-

nomic Theory,' *Journal of Political Economy*, Vol. 58, No. 3, June, pp. 211-221.

3. Bajt, A. (1968), 'Property in Capital and in the Means of Production in Socialist Economies,' *Journal of Law and Economics*, Vol. II, April, pp. 1-4.

4. Balfour, C. (1973), 'Workers' Participation in Western Europe,' in Balfour (ed.), *Participation in Industry*, London: Croom Helm (1973), pp. 181-212.

5. Bauer, O. (1921), *Der Weg zum Sozialismus*, Vienna.

6. Brittan, S. (1976), 'The Political Economy of British Union Monopoly Power,' *Three Banks Review*, Sept., No. 111, pp. 3-32.

7. Burton, J. (1983), 'Stagflation under Capitalist Liberal Democracy and Workers' Self-Management,' in J. Padioleau and A. Wolfelsperger (ed.), *The Economic Consequences of Democracy*, Paris: Editions de la Maison des Sciences de l'Homme (1983), forthcoming.

8. Burton, J., Hawkins, M. and Hughes, G. (1981), 'Is Liberal Democracy Especially Prone to Inflation? An Analytical Treatment,' in Hibbs and Fassbender (1981), *op. cit.*, pp. 249-268.

9. Cole, G.D.H., (1920a), *Self-Government in Industry*, London: Bell.

10. Cole, G.D.H., (1920b), *Guild Socialism: A Plan for Economic Democracy*, New York: F.A. Stokes.

11. Congdon, T. (1975), 'The Economics of Industrial Democracy,' *New Society*, Oct. 30, 1975, pp. 258-259.

12. Connock, M. (1973), 'How Workers in Yugoslavia Manage Lame Duck Industries,' *The Guardian*, Aug. 31, 1973.

13. Domar, E. (1966), 'The Soviet Collective Farm as a Producer Co-operative,' *American Economic Review*, Vol. 56, No. 4, Sept., Part I, pp. 734-757.

14. Heathfield, D.F. (ed.), (1977), *The Economics of Co-determination*, London: Macmillan.

15. Hibbs, D.A. Jr., and Fassbender, H.O. (1981), *Contemporary Political Economy: Studies of the Interdependence of Economics and Politics*, Amsterdam: North-Holland.

16. Hughes, G., Hawkins, M. and Burton, J. (1981), 'Inflation and Electoral Competition: A Comparative Analy-

sis,' *Review of International Studies*, Vol. 7, No. 4, Oct., pp. 199-216.

17. Jay, P. (1976), *A General Hypothesis of Employment, Inflation and Politics*, London: Institute of Economic Affairs, Occasional Paper 46.

18. Jay, P. (1977), 'Englanditis,' in R.E. Tyrell, Jr., (ed.), *The Future that Doesn't Work: Social Democracy's Failures in Britain*, New York: Doubleday (1977), pp. 167-185.

19. Johnson, A.G. and Whyte, W.F. (1977), 'The Mondragon System of Worker Production Co-operatives,' *Industrial and Labor Relations Review*, Oct., pp. 18-30.

20. Kosta, J. (1977), 'Workers' Councils in the Prague Spring of 1968,' in Heathfield, (1977), *op.cit.*, pp. 61-79.

21. Lindblom, C.E. (1949), *Unions and Capitalism*, New Haven: Yale University Press.

22. Martin, D.L. (1980), *An Ownership Theory of the Trade Union*, Berkeley: University of California Press.

23. Meade, J.E. (1972), 'The Theory of Labour-Managed Firms and of Profit-Sharing,' *Economic Journal*, Vol. 82, March, No. 325(S), pp. 402-428.

24. Moore, J.H. (1980), *Growth with Self-Management: Yugoslav Industrialization, 1952-1975*, Stanford.

25. Moore, J.H. (1981), 'Some Characteristics of the New Yugoslav Self-Management System,' Emory University: Law and Economics Center, (mimeo).

26. Oakeshott, R. (1975), 'Mondragon: Spain's Oasis of Democracy,' in Vanek (1975a), *op.cit.*, pp. 290-296.

27. O'Mahoney, D. (1979), 'Labour Management and the Market Economy,' *Journal of Irish Business and Administrative Research*, Vol. 1, No. 1, April, pp. 16-41.

28. Sapir, A. (1980), 'Economic Growth and Factor Substitution: What Happened to the Yugoslav Miracle?,' *Economic Journal*, Vol. 90, No. 358, June, pp. 294-313.

29 Vanek, J. (1969), 'Decentralization Under Workers' Management: A Theoretical Appraisal,' *American Economic Review*, Vol. 59, No. 5, pp. 1006-1014.

30. Vanek, J. (1970), *The General Theory of Labor-Managed Market Economies*, Ithaca: Cornell University Press.

31. Vanek, J. (1971), *The Participatory Economy: An Evolutionary Hypothesis and a Strategy for Development*, Ithaca: Cornell University Press.
32. Vanek, J. (1972), *The Economics of Workers' Management: A Yugoslav Case-Study*, London: Allen and Unwin.
33. Vanek, J. (1975a), (ed.), *Self-Management: Economic Liberation of Man, Selected Readings*, Harmondsworth, Middlesex: Penguin.
34. Vanek, J. (1975b), 'The Basic Theory of Financing of Participatory Firms,' in Vanek (1975a), *op.cit.*, pp. 445-455.
35. Ward, B. (1958), 'The Firm in Illyria: Market Syndicalism,' *American Economic Review*, Vol. 48, No. 4, Sept., pp. 566-589.

CHAPTER SIX

1. Addison, J.T. (1982a), 'Trade Unions and Restrictive Practices,' in J.J. Rosa (ed.), *op. cit.*, forthcoming.
2. Addison, J.T. (1982b), 'U.S. Unionism,' *Policy Review*, Winter, 1982, No. 9, pp. 7-8.
3. Alchian, A., and Demsetz, H. (1972), 'Production, Information Costs, and Economic Organization,' *American Economic Review*, Vol. 62, Dec., pp. 777-795.
4. Bellante, D. and Long, J. (1981), 'The Political Economy of the Rent-Seeking Society: The Case of Public Employees and their Unions,' *Journal of Labor Research*, Vol. II, No. 1, Spring, pp. 1-14.
5. Bennett, J.T. and Johnson, M.H. (1981), 'Union Use of Employee Pension Funds: Introduction and Overview,' *Journal of Labor Research*, Vol. II, No. 2, pp. 181-190.
6. Bloch, F.E. (1980), 'Political Support for Minimum Wage Legislation,' *Journal of Labor Research*, Vol. I, No. 2, Fall, pp. 245-253.
7. Brown, C. and Medoff, J. (1978), 'Trade Unions in the Production Process,' *Journal of Political Economy*, Vol. 86, No. 3, June, pp. 355-378.
8. Buchanan, J.M. (1975), *The Limits of Liberty*, Chicago: University of Chicago Press.
9. Burton, J. (1979), *The Trojan Horse: Union*

Power in British Politics, London: Adam Smith Institute.

10. Burton, J. (1980), 'A Discussion Paper in Political Economy: Some Further Reflections on Syndicalism,' *Government Union Review*, Vol. I, Spring, pp. 42-56.

11. Burton, J. (1982), Heritage Foundation: Washington, D.C., Heritage Lecture Series.

12. Burton, J. (1983), 'The Economic Analysis of the Trade Union as a Political Institution,' in J.J. Rosa (ed.), *op. cit.*, forthcoming.

13. Freeman, R.B. and Medoff, J.L. (1979), 'The Two Faces of Unionism,' *The Public Interest*, Fall, pp. 69-93.

14. Freeman, R.B. and Medoff, J.H. (1982), 'Comment,' *Policy Review*, Spring, 1982, No. 16, pp. 3-6.

15. Freeman, R.B. and Medoff, J.L. (1983), 'The Impact of Collective Bargaining: Illusion or Reality?,' *New Approaches to Labor Unions* (ed. J. Reid), Supplement to *Research in Labor Economics*, forthcoming.

16. Hirschman, A.O. (1970), *Exit, Voice and Loyalty*, Cambridge, Mass.: Harvard University Press.

17. Kau, J.B. and Rubin, P.H. (1978), 'Voting on Minimum Wages: A Time Series Analysis,' *Journal of Political Economy*, Vol. 86, No. 2 (1), April, pp. 337-432.

18. Kau, J.B. and Rubin, P.H. (1981), 'The Impact of Labor Unions on the Passage of Economic Legislation,' *Journal of Labor Research*, Vol. 2, No. 1, Spring, pp. 133-145.

19. Kurth, M.L. (1983), 'Public Employee Unions as Political Firms,' *New Approaches to Labor Unions* (ed. J. Reid), Supplement to *Research in Labor Economics*, forthcoming.

20. Martin, D.L. (1980), *An Ownership Theory of the Trade Union*, Berkeley: University of California Press.

21. McKenzie, R.B. (1980), 'The Labor Market Effects of Minimum Wage Laws: A New Perspective,' *Journal of Labor Research*, Vol. I, No. 2, Fall, pp. 255-264.

22. Olson, M. (1965), *The Logic of Collective Action*, Cambridge, Mass.: Harvard University Press.

23. Olson, M. (1982), *The Rise and Decline of Nations*, New Haven, Conn., Yale University Press.
24. Orr, D., (1976), 'Public Employee Compensation Levels, in A.L. Chickering (ed.), *Public Employee Unions*, San Francisco: Institute for Contemporary Studies, 1976, pp. 131-144.
25. Parsley, C.J. (1980), 'Labor Union Effects on Wage Gains: A Survey of Recent Literature,' *Journal of Economic Literature*, Vol. XVIII, March, No. 1, pp. 1-31.
26. Pencavel, J.H. (1977), 'The Distributional and Efficiency Effects of Trade Unions in Britain,' *British Journal of Industrial Relations*, Vol. 15, No. 2, July, pp. 137-156.
27. Reynolds, M.O. (1981), 'Whatever Happened to the Monopoly Model of Trade Unions?,' *Journal of Labor Research*, Vol. 2.
28. Rosa, J.J. (1983), *The Economics of Trade Unions – New Directions*, Amsterdam: Kluwer-Nijhoff.
29. Simons, H.C. (1944), 'Some Reflections on Syndicalism,' *Journal of Political Economy*, Vol. LII, March, No. 1, pp. 1-25.
30. Simons, H.C. (1980), 'Some Reflections on Syndicalism,' *Journal of Labor Research*, Spring, Reprint Series, No. 2, pp. 1-26.
31. Summers, C.W. (1974), 'Public Employee Bargaining: A Political Perspective,' *Yale Law Journal*, Vol. 83, pp. 1156-1200.
32. Troy, L., Koeller, C.T. and Sheflin, N. (1980), 'The Three Faces of Unionism,' *Policy Review*, Fall, pp. 95-109.

INDEX

Alienation, 104, 106-107
    see also Market syndicalism
Anglo-American Council on Productivity, 48
Atomic energy, 2
Attack on Inflation, 83, 87

Bargaining
    see Collective bargaining
Britain, xi-xii, 1-4, 27, 41, 58-59, 72, 102
    economy, 1-2, 5
    and European Economic Community, 2, 47
    first industrial nation, 1-2, 8
British disease, xii-xiii, xxi-xxii, 1-24, 47, 59, 66-69, 71, 103,
        108-109, 119-122, 126-127, 130
      defined, xii, 4, 6-7
      and economic growth performance, 5-9, 47, 67
      and government, 6
      popular view, 9-10
      and trade union movement, xiii, 4-5, 9, 60
    see also Capitalism; Economic growth; Inflation; Stagflation;
        Trade union movement; Unemployment; Western economies
British Rail, 62-63
Bullock Committee of Inquiry on Industrial Democracy, 87

Canada, xi, xiii
    economy, 49, 131
Canadian Labour Congress, xiii
Capitalism, xix, 74-75, 101, 103-106, 108, 110-112, 114-115,
        117, 122-124, 126
    survival of, 129-154
Captive
    see Capture process
Capture process, xxiv, 141, 153
Cartel(s), 12-14, 80, 135-136, 140-145
Civil Service Pay Research Unit, 35
Closed shop, 14, 64-65, 84-86, 139, 148
Coal industry (Britain), 14-15, 20, 58, 86
Collective
    action, xiv-xv, 54-55, 63, 149, 152
    bargaining, 27-28, 35, 47-49, 52, 54-55, 57,
        64-66, 72-74, 82-83, 92-93, 109, 144, 146
    voice, 54-57, 134-135, 143
Collective Bargaining and the Social Contract, 83
Competition, 14, 19, 22, 139, 141
Concertation, 78

Concordat
    see Social Contract
Consumer, 107, 115, 118, 141, 145, 150-152
    interests, xvii, xxi, 79, 87, 107, 126
    price index, xix, xxiv-xxv, 94
Contestation, 78
Contracts
    see Long-term contracts
Contractual Organisation of Associated Labour, 117
Corporatism, xvii-xviii, 71-101, 150-151
Cost, xiv, 26
Cult of the amateur, 6, 8

Deficit finance, 16-17, 23, 36, 40-41, 43, 80-81
Demand, 28-29, 32-34, 36-37, 76
    curve, 14
    for inflation, xiv, 11, 40, 119
Democracy,
    see Capitalism
Deregulation, 1-2
Development of the Social Contract, 83

Economic growth, xiv-xvi, 2, 5-10, 47-69
    in Britain, 1, 5-7, 21, 47-48, 67
    and market syndicalism, 125-126
    sluggish, xii-xiii, 2, 5-9, 19-23, 47-48, 150
    and trade unions, 21-22, 47-69
Economic evolution, 2, 20-22, 67, 126-127
Efficiency, 5, 19
    see also Static allocative inefficiency effect;
        Static X-inefficiency effect
Employment, xiii, 8, 13, 39-40, 108-109
    see also Unemployment
Endogenous systems, 96
Englanditis, 2
    see also British disease
English sickness, 2, 4
    see also British disease
Entrepreneur(s), xxi, 2, 112-117, 125-127, 129, 142, 144-145, 151
    and Market syndicalism, 112-116, 126-127
Equity, xvii, 73-75, 82, 115-116
European Commission, 102
European Economic Community, 2, 4, 48
Exit option, 138-139, 145
    see also Voice option

Firms, xix, xxi, 16, 38, 59, 112-114, 142
    new firms, 112-114, 125
France, 2, 4, 49

Free enterprise, 2
Free rider, xvii, 15, 63, 72-74, 88
Free trade, 2
Fundamental determinant, xiv, 11, 25, 38-41, 45-46, 77
      see also Proximate determinant
Furnace theory, 10-11, 26-28, 30, 34, 36-37, 39, 82-83

Go-slows,
      see Strikes
Government
      bureaucracy, 44
      demand, 12
      legislation, 27, 83-89, 102, 133, 150
      monetary expansion, 11, 16, 23
      regulation, 15, 75, 130
      subsidies, 14-15, 21-22, 63, 146
Gross Domestic Product
      see Gross National Product
Gross National Product, 4, 20, 48, 74, 91, 94

Harvard School, xiv-xv, xxiv, 47, 53, 55-58, 60, 136-138, 144-145, 147

In Place of Strife, 88
Income(s)
      policy, 35, 62, 71-73, 81, 85, 89
      redistribution, 12, 16-17, 35, 52
Industrial democracy
      see Market syndicalism
Inflation, xii-xiv, 6-11, 16-17, 22-23, 26-46, 71, 73, 76-79, 81-84, 91,
      94-97, 108-109, 119-121, 126, 130
      demand for, 11, 16, 40
      determinants of, 38-39, 45-46, 97
      indirect taxation, xvi, 16-17
      price, xviii, 9, 26-27, 37, 42-43, 81, 95-96
      sociopolitical view, 71-73
      wage, xx, 9-11, 26-29, 37-38, 44-45
      see also British disease; Trade union movement
Interest groups
      see Special interest groups
Interest rates, 16
Invisible hand, 134

Keynesian school, 10, 16-17, 129
      and full employment, 40, 108

Labour, 51, 53, 55, 78
      costs, 9
      market, xi-xiii, 11, 18, 26, 32, 37-38, 88, 111, 140-142
      productivity, 49-50

Index

Legislation
    see Government, legislation
Leviathan model, 44-45
Lobby(ies), xxv, 11, 15, 22-23, 40, 126, 146
Local Government, Planning and Land Act, 65
Long-term contract, 33

Manufacturing, 1, 6
Market escape, xxv, 141, 150-153
Market revolution, 2
Market syndicalism, xix, xxi, 101-127, 150-151
    and alienation, 104, 106-107
    and British disease, xx, 103, 107-108, 119-122, 126-127
    defined, xix, 103-104
    and guild socialism, 108-109
    sociopolitical factors, 104-105
    and usufruct property right, 103-104
    in Yugoslavia, xix, 102, 104, 112, 115, 120-122, 124, 126
Meidner Plan, 98
Militancy,
    see Trade union, militancy
Minimum wage
    see Wage, minimum
Monetarism, xx, 9, 25-26, 36-37, 43, 74, 77, 108
Money supply, 26, 38-39, 41-43, 80, 83, 108
Monopoly, xx, 12, 52, 63, 85, 98, 116-117, 135-137, 140-141,
    143, 146-147, 151-152
    power, 12, 19, 27-28, 89-91, 108, 110-111, 123, 131-132, 152
    rent, 12-14, 110-111

National Board for Prices and Incomes, 61
National Coal Board, 14
National Economic Development Office, 48
National Labour Relations Board, 142

Occupational striation, 64-65
Oil price hike, 96
Organization for Economic Cooperation and Development, 8
Output, 6, 20, 25, 38, 45, 55, 58, 61, 92, 108, 123, 135
    loss, 6, 52-53

Pecuniary market, 12-13, 17, 81-82, 110, 122, 148
Phillips curve, 9, 11
Political market, xiii, 4, 11-12, 14-17, 21-23, 43, 68-69, 76,
    80, 92-93, 99, 110, 122, 136-137, 145-149
Price, 26-28, 34, 42-43, 61, 81, 84, 95-96, 108, 111,
    controls, 79
    inflation, 9, 26, 37, 81, 84, 94-95
Prisoner's dilemma, 72, 74, 82, 99, 134, 152

Private sector, 28, 36
Producer, xxv, 76, 79, 141, 150, 152
  lobby, 15-16, 21-22, 76, 98
  and market syndicalism, 107, 110-111, 118-119, 126
  power, 76, 98, 110
Product market, xxi, 32, 36, 63
Production, 2, 98
  means of, xxi
Productivity, xv-xvi, 5, 8-10, 20-21, 47-69, 106, 143-145
  bargaining, 52, 60-62, 64-66
  management, 51-52, 55
Profits, xv, xix, 12, 28, 59, 78, 112, 123, 143-145
Proximate determinant, 10, 25-27, 38, 40, 45-46, 77, 83, 108
  see also Fundamental determinant
Public choice, 43, 67, 98
Public sector, 28, 35-36, 43-44, 62, 84-92, 146

Reagan administration, 15-16
Rent-seeking, 12, 14, 16, 80, 110-111
Resource allocation, 17, 58-60, 67
Restrictive practices, 10, 20, 22, 49, 60, 65
Sectional interest groups
  see Special interest groups
Shock effect, 54, 57, 68
Sick Man of Europe, 2
  see also British disease
Sluggish growth
  see Economic growth
Social contract, xviii, xxvi, 72, 83-85, 87-91
Sociopolitical analysis, 71, 75, 104-105
Soviet bloc, 102
Special interest groups, xiii-iv, xvi-xix, xxi, xxv-xxvi, 21
  23-24, 44-46, 67-68, 71-72, 77, 80, 108-111, 118-119,
  134, 150-151, 153
Spillover, 27, 30-31, 34-35
  agnostic, 33
Stagflation, xx, 6-8, 108-109, 129-130
Standard Oil, 61
Static allocative inefficiency effect, 20-23, 60
Static X-inefficiency effect, 20-23
Sterling devaluation, 7
Strike(s), 5, 49, 51, 66, 77, 84, 88, 90-95, 97, 111, 130-132
Strike threat power, xxiii, 28, 131-132
Subsidies
  see Government, subsidies
Supply, 12, 40, 119

Taxpayers, 15, 28, 36. 80

Thatcher government, 7, 15
Trade Disputes Act, 88
Trade Union Congress, 83-85, 87-89
Trade Union and Labour Relations Act, 85-86
Trade union movement, xi-xiii
    and British disease, 1-24
    density, 28-29, 33, 46, 55, 58, 64, 68, 91-94, 142
    in Canada, xi
    as cause of unemployment, 17-19, 39-40
    and market syndicalism, 101-127
    militancy, 9-10, 27-30
    monopoly, 19, 27-28, 52-53, 85-89, 108-112, 131-132, 135, 146-147
    power, xxiii, xxvi, 18-19, 27-28, 88, 98, 118-119, 130-131
    reform, 5, 83, 88-89
    spillover, 27, 30-32, 35
    union-non-union differentials, 18, 27, 29-30, 33-34, 46, 52, 90-91
Tripartitism
    see Corporatism

Unemployment, xii-xiii, xviii-xx, 6-9, 11, 17-19, 22-23, 26, 35-40, 44,
    62-74, 90, 93, 95-96, 108-109, 123-124, 126

Voice option, 138-139
    see also Exit option

Wage, 11, 18, 22-23, 30, 32-34, 36-38, 40-44, 52-53, 56, 62, 77, 123-124, 144
    demands, 5, 17-18, 32-37
    differentials, 13, 54, 29-30, 54
    floors, 18-19, 23
    inflation, xvii, 9-11, 26-30, 37-38, 41, 46, 73-74, 79-81, 95
    minimum, xxv, 18, 34, 123, 146, 151
    push, 10, 27-29, 40-42, 81, 90
    real, 96
    restraint, 72-74, 82
    replacement ratio, 18-19
    spillover, 31-32, 36
West Germany, 2, 4, 7, 48-49, 102, 104
Western economies, xi-xii, xx-xxii, xxvi, 2, 6-9, 102-105, 108, 120, 124, 129
White Paper, 83-84, 87-88, 104
Workers self-management
    see Market syndicalism

Yugoslavia, xix, xxi, 101-102, 104, 112, 115-116, 120-122, 124